Globalisation and the Changing Face of Port Infrastructure

Prabir De

Globalisation and the Changing Face of Port Infrastructure

The Indian Perspective

PETER LANG
Bern · Berlin · Bruxelles · Frankfurt am Main · New York · Oxford · Wien

Bibliographic information published by Die Deutsche Bibliothek
Die Deutsche Bibliothek lists this publication in the Deutsche Nationalbibliografie; detailed bibliographic data is available on the Internet at ‹http://dnb.ddb.de›.

British Library Cataloguing-in-Publication Data: A catalogue record for this book is available from The British Library, Great Britain

Library of Congress Cataloging-in-Publication Data

De, Prabir.
Globalisation and the changing face of port infrastructure : the Indian perspective / Prabir De. – 1st ed.
p. cm.
ISBN 978-3-0343-0005-6 (alk. paper)
1. Harbors–India. 2. Harbors–Economic aspects–India. I. Title.
HE559.I4D4 2009
387.10954–dc22

2009023843

Cover illustrations: © by Prabir De

Cover design: Eva Rolli, Peter Lang AG

ISBN 978-3-0343-0005-6

Hochfeldstrasse 32, CH-3012 Bern
info@peterlang.com, www.peterlang.com, www.peterlang.net

To my parents

Contents

Preface

This book is an attempt to understand the process of India's port sector development in the era of globalisation. It quantitatively evaluates the structural metamorphosis in Indian port industry covering a period of almost two decades and a half. The main emphasis of this book is on performance evaluation, technological change, productivity, inequality, and market concentration in Indian port sector. Another protracted objective of the book is to create a ground for discussion on various aspects of port infrastructure and the resultant policy action.

This volume makes an original contribution in three respects: firstly, performance of Indian ports, for the first time, has been scientifically investigated. The issue of causality between performance and traffic in Indian ports has been dealt elaborately; secondly, the port industry was analysed through the application of total factor productivity (TFP) growth. The inequality among the ports and the competition aspect were also analysed explicitly; and finally, the results of the research undoubtedly provide governments, port authorities and other stakeholders with information and guidelines for improving the country's port infrastructure.

The message of this book has immense importance at a time when Indian port industry is passing through a very crucial phase due to restructuring of the Indian economy in general and global trade in particular; a time when one group of people are applauding success while a large opponents are questioning whether the sector can ensure stability of returns and sustenance of the India's globalisation programme. However, there is a general consensus that inadequacies in port infrastructure are a bottleneck to growth, a threat to competitiveness, and an obstacle to trade-led globalisation. This study examines major challenges and issues in improving India's port infrastructure.

Stimulating interaction with a diverse and extremely lively group of individuals over the last decade and a half made me feel the lack of a readily available text that covered with reasonable rigour and manageable detail the complex issues surrounding India's port infrastructure. I owe debt of gratitude to many individuals for their comments, suggestions and encouragements. They saved me from errors and encouraged me to carry on with this project. In particular, I am indebted to Buddhadeb Ghosh of the Indian Statistical Institute (Kolkata), who being co-author of some of the papers adopted in this book was instrumental in putting me to the field of maritime economics. I am particularly thankful to Arvind Kumar, S B Das, Dilip Halder, Arindam Banik, and Srikumar Ghosh for their suggestions and encouragements. I am thankful to my institute, and the Director General for letting me to do this work. At Peter Lang Publishing Group, I am grateful to Stephan Moser and Martina Fierz for their sincere guidance and support. I thank Pradeep Kumar who did an excellent type-setting of the manuscript. Finally, I cannot adequately thank my wife, Mistu, and my daughter, Mahasweta, who provided critical emotional and intellectual support during the period this book was written.

Prabir De

List of Tables, Figures and Appendices

Tables

Figures

Appendices

List of Abbreviations

APM	A P Moller
BOR	Berth Occupancy Rate
BOT	Build, Operate, and Transfer
BTR	Berth Throughput Rate
CCT	Chennai Container Terminal
cif	Cost, Insurance, and Freight
COSCO	China Ocean Shipping Company
CV	Coefficient of Variation
DMU	Decision Making Unit
DPI	Dubai Ports International
DPW	Dubai Ports World
FERA	Foreign Exchange Regulation Act
fob	Free on Board
GRT	Gross Registered Tonnage
HHI	Herfindahl-Hirschman Index
HPH	Hutchison Port Holdings
IDFC	Infrastructure Development Finance Company
IPA	Indian Ports Association
JNPT	Jawaharlal Nehru Port Trust
LDC	Least Developed Country
LP	Labour Productivity
MNC	Multinational Corporations
MRTP	Monopolistic and Restrictive Trade Practices Act
MT	Million Tonnes
NMDP	National Maritime Development Progromme
NMP	National Maritime Policy
NSICT	Nava Sheva International Container Terminal
OLS	Ordinary Least Squares
OSBD	Output per Ship Berth Day
PBWT	Pre-Berthing Waiting Time

PCA	Principal Component Analysis
POL	Petroleum, Oil and Lubricants
PPI	Port Performance Index
PPP	Public – Private Partnership
PSA	Port of Singapore Authority
R&D	Research and Development
RRT	Rate of Return on Turnover
SD	Standard Deviation
SEE	Standard Error of Estimate
SSA	Stevedoring Services of America
TAMP	Tariff Authority of Major Ports of India
TEU	Twenty-foot Equivalent Unit
TFP	Total Factor Productivity
TRT	Turn-Round Time
UNCTAD	United Nations Conference on Trade and Development
WTO	World Trade Organisation

Introduction

The kinship between economics and geographical factors is consanguineous. It is easy to understand but difficult to establish empirically. It is the ultimate reality. This was well recognised by both the classical economists like Adam Smith, and the pioneers of development economics like Myrdal and Hirschman. Smith's emphasis on geography goes through the transport mechanism which strengthens his classic sequence of division of labour followed by productivity and specialisation with market expansion in a free trade regime in the period of globalisation.

> As by means of water-carriage a more extensive market is opened to every sort of industry than what land-carriage alone can afford it, so it is upon sea-coast, and along the banks of navigable rivers, that industry of every kind naturally begins to subdivide and improve itself, and it is frequently not till a long time after that those improvements extend themselves to the inland part of the country.[1]

At another point, Smith's reference to India (and Bengal) is reminiscent of our past trading glory.

> There are in Africa none of those great inlets, such as the Baltic and Adriatic seas in Europe, the Mediterranean and Euxine seas in both Europe and Asia, and the gulfs of Arabia, Persia, India and Bengal, and Siam, in Asia, to carry maritime commerce into the interior parts of that great continent.[2]

Until eighties of the last century economists did not deal directly with such factors as transportation and ports, manufacturing belt and urbanisation which clearly exemplified the operation of 'increasing returns'. Thus, till the other day, the relationship was rather asymmetric.

1 Cited in Radelet and Sachs (1998).
2 Ibid.

For example, economic geographers, while constructing their analytical theories and explanations of unbalanced regional development, have drawn freely on the prevailing concepts of economics. But economists have tended to accord little, if any, attention to geographical factors in economic modelling even when they fail to find any economic justification for the same. The traditional logic, that counters this argument, points to the price mechanism that is supposed to take care of the forces of supply and demand. But, it awfully fails to answer the problems of specialisation, trade orientation, increasing returns and hence, regional inequality. Even if it does, price is all-inclusive there, leaving no role for the non-price factors (e.g. transport). The whole host of international trade economists have termed the national economy as 'spaceless' (Krugman, 1998). 'Space' or what may be called 'geography' is so important that it can neatly divide the world into some basic building blocks. For example, there are on the whole 44 landlocked countries in the world, out of which except only a handful of European countries like Austria and Switzerland, the remaining countries are neither developed nor rich in terms of per capita income. These handful of countries (seven only) are located in Western Europe, and hence deeply integrated into the developed European space. This is perhaps one of the causes for the commonly held view that poverty is by and large 'tropical' (Gallup and Sachs, 1998). Moreover, a significant share of the population in the developed countries is concentrated in the coastal region. By sharp contrast, the population living in South Asia is heavily concentrated in the interior. Specifically, India's great mass of population live along the course of the Ganges until very recently. Most of these habitations are often hundreds of kilometres away from the coast. Among others, this aptly demonstrates our inward-looking attitude. For example, even in those states that have a very high coastal line, the main centres of economic activity are located in the hinterland.

It is worthwhile to mention here that nearly 200 years after Johann Von Thunen's 'Isolated State' (1826), seventy years after Alfred Weber's 'Theory of Location of Industries' (1929), fifty years after August Losch's 'The Economics of Location' (1954), and Walter Isard's 'Location and the Space Economy' (1956) have been published, nowhere in the world spatial factors like transportation (and more specifically, port), regional inequality and urbanisation have found any place in any economics textbooks.

Before switching to the theme of the book let us have a brief recapitulation of the logic behind the rise of this 'new economic geography'.[3] In the standard neo-classical formulation, there is a natural smooth tendency towards inter-regional transmission of growth from the richer to the poorer regions within an economy with perfect mobility of factors and diminishing returns to capital. Barro and Sala-i-Martin (1995), Quah (1993) and many others have tried to test the hypothesis of convergence of economic growth or levels of economic development as between different regions within a country as also between different advanced countries themselves. But this theorisation pays little attention away from the conventional wisdom to the spatial variables which, for all practical purposes, have significant influence on the process of economic development, trade and technology orientation.[4]

A parallel literature in economic geography has been simultaneously trying to enrich the explanatory power of the regional development theory incorporating the impact of external sector on domestic economic development more specifically. Thus, over the past two decades a 'new trade theory' and a 'new economics of competitive advantage' have emerged which brought to the forefront the role that the internal geographical factors of an economy have played in determining the trading performance of that economy's industries as well as concentration / spread of economic activity.[5] In this endeavour, Paul Krugman, the leading exponent of the 'new trade theory' has sought to answer how interna-

3 For a critical and comprehensive review see Martin (1999).

4 Beyond this convergence syndrome Indian economic development during the last few decades displays rather a tendency towards divergence across the major regions (Marjit and Mitra, 1996; Ghosh, Marjit and Neogi, 1998; Dasgupta et al., 2000).

5 This new and popular wave of research works in the fields of 'new trade theory' and 'new economic geography' was pioneered in a series of seminal works which started about two decades ago: Dixit and Stiglitz (1977), Lancaster (1980), Krugman (1979, 1981), Porter (1990), Fujita et al. (1999).

tional trade of a country is both influenced by and in turn influences the process of geographical distribution of economic activities within a nation (Krugman, 1991, 1993, 1995). In a different but related vein, Porter (1990) has argued that the degree of geographical clustering of industries within an economy plays an important role in determining which of its sectors command a 'competitive advantage' within the global economy. Thus, in order to understand the trading performance of a country, we need to know its nature of supply of the trading instruments from the points of production to the final outlet in the chain of transportation. This may be reflected in differing economic performance of various competing regions. Thus, the linkage from the production centres to the final destinations through various transaction points in the chain of location is a very central theme of the process by which economic prosperity and trade are created and maintained in the era of globalisation.

In a recent work, Fink, Mattoo and Neagu (2002) have argued with US data that maritime transport costs significantly impede international trade. They examine why these costs are so high in some countries and quantify the importance of two explanations: restrictive trade policies and private anti-competitive practices. This paper finds that both are important, but the latter have a greater impact. Trade liberalisation and the break up of private carrier agreements would lead to an average of one-third lower liner transport prices and to cost savings of upto US$ 3 billion on goods carried to the United States alone. The policy implications for such studies are very close to the present one: there is a need not only for further liberalisation of government policy but also for strengthening international disciplines on restrictive business practices.

Relating to transportation and trade, Limao and Venables (2001) have investigated the dependence of transport costs on geography and infrastructure facilities. Hummels (1999a, 1999b) found for the United States that the *ad valorem* transport cost is 7.6 percent for food and live animals, but only 2.25 percent for machinery and transport equipment. Table 1.1 gives some indications of this transport cost measure for various countries.

Table 1.1 Cif/Fob Ratio, 1965–1990

Country	Cif/fob ratio (%)	Country	Cif/fob ratio (%)
Australia	10.3	New Zealand	11.5
Australia	4.1	Norway	2.7
Canada	2.7	Philippines	7.6
Denmark	4.5	Portugal	10.3
France	4.2	Singapore	6.1
West Germany	3.0	Spain	6.4
Greece	13.0	Sweden	3.5
Ireland	5.0	Switzerland	1.8
Italy	7.1	Thailand	11.0
Japan	9.0	United Kingdom	6.0
Netherlands	5.6	United States	4.9

Source: Cited in Radelet and Sachs (1998)

The difference in shipping costs can be explained by noting that countries located further away from major markets face higher shipping costs (for example, New Zealand), and by observing whether or not countries are landlocked. For example, the landlocked developing countries have on average 50 percent higher transport costs than coastal developing economics (Radelet and Sachs, 1998). These authors also find that for developing countries a doubling of trading cost reduces economic growth by 0.5 percent. As argued above, these figures probably underestimate true costs. Hummels (1999a) finds that freight rates differ substantially over exporters. However, expenditures on freight are at 'the low end of the range.' This suggests that these costs are substantial and that import choices are made to minimise transport costs. Note that products with very high transport costs are not even traded at all. Hummels (1999b) also shows that, in contrast to popular opinion, transport costs have not declined uniformly. His general conclusions are that in the post World War II period, the costs of ocean travel have increased and the costs of air travel have fallen, and that the costs of distant travel have fallen relative to proximate travel (Hummels, 2007).

For a final indication of the importance of transport costs, we can compare freight costs with other trade costs, like tariffs. For the

USA, Davis (1998) finds that industry-level transport costs as a percentage of imports range between 1.9 percent and 8.5 percent of import values, with a mean of 4.8 percent. Industry-level tariff ranged from 0.5 percent to 15.4 percent with a mean of 4.1 percent. Transport costs, therefore, seem to be at least as important as policy-induced trade barriers.

Now that we have seen that transport costs between and within countries are substantial (Hummles, 2009), one might ask whether or not they matter. The answer is: they do. Limao and Venables (2001) find that transport costs are very important in the ability of countries to participate in the global economy. The tendency towards trade liberalisation makes transport costs such relatively more important than the official trade barriers, like tariffs. Using various econometric techniques they find that the elasticity of trade with respect to transport costs is high, approximately equal to –2.65. This implies, for example, that a median landlocked country has only about 30 percent of the trade flows that a coastal country has. Being landlocked raises transport cost by around 50 percent. Moreover, Limao and Venables find that the relatively poor quality of sub-Saharan African infrastructure is to a large extent responsible for the relatively low level of African trade with the rest of the world. Finally, it must be noted that distance not only has a physical representation, but also a mental element.

What follows is that infrastructure appears to be an important determinant of transport costs – international or otherwise. Moreover, analyses of bilateral trade data confirm the importance of infrastructure, and give an estimate of the elasticity of trade flows with respect to trade cost factor of around -2.65 (Limao and Venables, 2001). The above findings have direct connotation for Indian port sector, which alone carries 85 percent of India's merchandise trade.

In India, awareness towards the impact of port infrastructure on economic development in general and international trade in particular has increased only in recent years partly as a result of numerous reports regarding the fragile state of the country's port infrastructure. The importance of efficient port for the growth of the international trade stems from the chain linkage between production, performance of individual ports and overseas transportation leading to exports ever since the liberal economic regime initiated in 1991.[6]

Traditional trade and development theories try to explain export growth of a developing country in terms of price competitiveness of exportable. There rarely exists any literature on export promotion which focuses on the role played by different non-price factors and that too, the factors which are not related with physical process of production but nonetheless affect the supply of exportable, such as administrative process, government rules and regulations, infrastructural bottlenecks, among others. These factors imply that an exporting firm must employ its own resources either in terms of 'time' or in terms of 'money' before the actual shipments of export items.

Export of a commodity is determined by its demand supply conditions. The mainstream economic theories strive to find out how the world market share of an export item from a particular country can be increased, ceteris paribus its global demand. Barring a few streams of thought, most of the mainstream analyses on export promotion stress the price-sensitive factors which affect both demand and supply of exports from an economy. They promote exports by increasing price competitiveness of the particular product vis-à-vis the rest of the world, and constitute the major planks of any trade policy reform in a developing economy in recent times.

But, studies which analyse the question of competitiveness of India's exports rigorously by segregating the price and non-price factors are rare. The necessity of such studies stems from the following reason. In

6 Public capital in port sector such as radio wireless station, pilot vessels, mooring boats, tugs, cranes and trailers of various types, warehousing and storage facilities, water supply and energy facilities, fire fighting utilities, conservancy, etc. could be viewed as inputs in the service process which contribute independently to the cargo handling. Under the present institutional set up, the role of private capital in Indian ports is very limited. Yet, it is generally taken for granted that decades of 'sheltered market' phenomenon has not created any 'outward looking' tendency in India. Moreover, high 'gestation lag' in the port sector is believed to be the main cause for low level of private capital in this sector even under the selective liberalisation initiated by the government in the post-1991 period.

the mainstream traditional analysis, export promotion is garnered through price measures by gearing up the price competitiveness of a particular product. The underlying presumption is that, the foreign demand for the product, enhanced through such measures, would automatically generate supply of it. That is to say, in traditional analysis, scant attention is paid to supply constraints of exports.

Supply constraints can be categorised as one directly linked with the physical process of production (e.g. technology), and also, as one not linked with the production process. The latter is mostly concerned with pre- and post-production process of exports and, give rise to what is known as 'transaction costs'.

The effects of poor port performance on a country's trade and transaction costs have become too obvious (Juhel, 1999). Inefficient ports, whether through lack of integrated transport network, outdated work practices or obsolete facilities, can stall a country's export growth and also increase the costs of transaction in a borderless world. The unreliability and poor quality of other complementary infrastructural services often add to the costs of production of exportables, and adversely affect a country's international competitiveness (Rauch, 1991). Rising inefficiencies in ports have forced the governments all over the world to deregulate the port system (Estache and Carbajo, 1997; Bollard and Pickford, 1998).[7] Many governments have began to deregulate economic activities, and decentralise decision making, with the objective of increasing financial viability and productive efficiency of the public sector. Towards this direction, governments across the world are presently reformulating the way they control, regulate, and manage ports, with the general principle of reducing direct intervention and where feasible, the use of the private sector for typical port operations is being introduced.

7 However, there is also result in opposite direction. In a study, Coto-Millan, et al. (2000) have shown that greater autonomy in management has generated greater economic inefficiency in Spanish ports during the period 1985-89. But such studies are limited by very time-specific issues, and hence should be evaluated continuously.

This book attempts to understand the role the port plays in India's economic development. The importance of this work has increased a lot ever since the initiation of India's globalisation programme of 1991. We have mainly dealt with performance indicators, technological changes, and labour productivities of major ports of India. This is an empirical study dealing with major ports of India, and covers a period of last quarter century.

1.1 Objective

This book addresses the aforesaid issues in the context of India. Several reasons explain the choice of the Indian port sector. First, the port sector in several erstwhile developing countries has been undergoing revolutionary transformation from a subsistence infrastructure resource into a more capital intensive, commercially oriented facility during the last two decades and a half. On the other hand, India has lately thought about taking some steps leading to deregulation of the country's port sector. Indian ports are currently characterised by the existence of obsolete and poorly maintained equipment, hierarchical and bureaucratic management structures, lack of transparency, weak coordination between the port authorities and users of the ports, lack of synchronisation of working times, excessive labour, and in general, an institutional framework that is considerably at variance with government's overall economic objectives (De Monie, 1995; Peters, 1997; Haralambides and Behrens, 2000; IDFC, 2001; De, 2003). Second, considering the country's entry into the second stage of reform, the analysis will help assess the potential benefits of moving to a deregularised port sector under a liberal trading regime when about 85 percent of the country's foreign trade pass through seaports. For instance, if performance stimulates traffic, then the benefits of performance augmenting factors might be responsible not only for redistribution of existing traffic but also for attracting new manufacturers/suppliers. There are ample examples to show that even if a country produces technologically advanced quality goods (pure theory of trade), non-price factors such as poor quality of infrastructure often work as decisive deterrence to participation in trade. Hence, causal inspection of trends of country's overseas trade suggests the need for an investigation into the relationship between port performance and port traffic. We also have to ascertain whether or not an efficient port raises the return of factors of production and profitability of the users of ports. For most of the developing countries like India, the role of port as a policy instrument for both higher mobility and lower transaction costs as well as for spreading the growth centres away from the core metropolitan location has not been utilised so far. The importance of such work has increased a lot ever since the initiation of our globalisation programme in 1991. Above all, one protracted objective of this study is to create a ground for discussion on various aspects of the topic under discussion and the resultant policy action.

1.2 Outline of the Book

This book attempts to assess the role that port plays in India's economic development. We have mainly dealt with performance indicators, technological changes, and labour productivities of major ports of India. This is an empirical study dealing with major ports of India, and covers a period of last quarter century. Most of the data have been collected from the Government sources. The choice of the period of this analysis, coverage of ports, sources of data, and methodology of analysis have been described in details in the respective chapters. The book has been organised in following chapters.

Chapter 1 (the present chapter) is the introductory chapter which includes in brief the research objectives, outline of the book, concept of port and related research, overview of the India's ports before and after Independence, institutional set-up, profile and performance of Indian ports, etc. with a view to define the perspective of the study.

Chapter 2 is concerned with the performance of Indian ports in terms of output growth corresponding to input growth. Individual performance of Indian ports, along with the construction of a port performance index (PPI) with the help of principal component analysis (PCA), is discussed. This chapter also tries to find out the relationship between port performance, labour endowment and the port traffic during the last quarter century. We have also tested the impact of port performance and labour endowment on port traffic.

Chapter 3 attempts to establish the relationship, if any, between performance and traffic of Indian ports over the period from 1985 to 2005. Investigating into this relationship may be highly useful in optimisation of resource allocation among the Indian ports. For instance, if performance stimulates traffic, then the benefits of performance augmenting factors might be responsible not only for redistribution of existing traffic but also for attracting new manufacturers/suppliers as well. Therefore, a causal inspection of trends of country's overseas trade suggests the need for an investigation into the linkages between port performance and port traffic.

Chapter 4 deals with the total factor productivity (TFP), which is a supposed measure of technological change in industry over time, of Indian ports. Here, we talk about two related approaches to the measurement of TFP, namely, the production function approach and the growth accounting approach (of national income) using some fixed shares of inputs. We use the first approach explicitly in terms of a Cobb-Douglas production function in this chapter.

Chapter 5 attempts to assess the effect of technological advancement as reflected in strictly rising capital intensities on the productivities of labour with the help of average production function. Here, we try to find out the effect of technological advancement as reflected in rising capital intensities on the productivity of labour in Indian ports. This chapter also identifies the factors influencing labour productivities in Indian ports.

Chapter 6 analyses the nature of competitive environment prevails in the Indian port sector using some standard tools of market concentration over time. Here, we measure of the degree of inter-port competition during the pre- and post-liberalisation period. The issue of inequality among Indian ports, whether or not as a resultant of improved performance, was also discussed in this chapter.

Here, we also deal with firm-level market concentration in Indian port industry. We investigate formal properties of rising concentration of container port system with particular reference to Indian private port terminals.

Finally, Chapter 7 presents a summary of the results along with possible policy implications and directions for further research.

1.3 Concept of Port and Related Studies

A port is essentially an economic concept, an economic infrastructure that serves to handle coastal and overseas traffic. Port is a sub-system of the total transport network and a meeting place of other modes of transport. A port is a gateway for the entrance from surface water to land and vice versa. Port is also construed as the major crossroad of traffic in ideas, peoples and goods over the centuries (Kindleberger, 1996).

There is sufficient evidence in the literature of a strong spatial relationship between transportation and economic development. It is universally recognised that capital formation has very direct and positive impact on growth. Among its various components, transportation is an important component of capital formation. The question of where economic activities should be located is partly determined by 'historical accidents' and partly by the geographical specificities of the country concerned— the motive force which guides economists to develop models of the spatial structure of the economy. Kurgman (1998) has also emphasised the lack of concern with the spatial perspective as evident in the ways in which geographic phenomena are spatially interconnected and the interaction that occurs over geographic space. In some works, Fujita and Mori (1995, 1996, 1997) have explained the evolutionary model of spatial economic development in which agglomeration economies and the hub-effect of transport nodes interplay in the making of major cities. Their model explains the irreversibility of spatial economic development such as the continuing prosperity of port cities even after initial advantage of water-access had become irrelevant. It is also shown that in order to decentralise industries from the core region to a periphery region, a temporary protection of industries in the periphery by worsening the transport connection with the core for a short period of time may be desirable. But their findings may not be necessarily true in case of an economy where port does not play a decisive role in the growth of the economy.[8]

The historic and most common view about the role of transportation in the development process is that it is a precondition for economic growth. While dealing with the stimulus to the take-off stage of economic growth in the US, Rostow (1964) identifies the railroads as the critical investment sector. According to Hunter (1965), the economic history of Western Europe and North America has shown that the introduction of modern transportation methods has drastically lowered shipping costs. There is a causal linkage between low-cost transportation and economic development. The industrial revolution was facilitated, among other things, by a prior revolution in transport technology. Some of the pioneering studies (Fogel, 1964; Cootner, 1963) have found that in terms of causal association, development of transportation facilities was the outcome of rising demand. That is, transport facilities were built-up in a process of 'backward linkage' of industrialisation. Hardly any attempt has been made in recent years to verify the impact of transport network on trade in the Least Developed Countries (LDCs). To the best of our knowledge, the work by Taaffe, Morrill and Gould (1963) is

8 A review of the literature suggests three possible relationships, with transportation having (i) a positive effect on the development process – the expansion in directly productive activities being a direct result of providing improved transportation facilities, (ii) a permissive effect on the development process, because transportation does not independently produce directly productive activities or subsequent increases in the level of economic growth, (iii) a negative effect occurring when an over investment in transportation reduces potential growth in directly productive activity, and consequently leads to an absolute decline in the level of income per capita (Goutheir, 1970).

such an attempt for understanding the transport network and development in West Africa.

Apart from the aforesaid role of transportation in economic development, Samuelson (1954) in a classic paper dealt with the effects of trade impediments as a result of transport bottleneck under a 2x2 framework. But considering the exact location of production unit of the exportable item in the home country thereby making 'distance' an explicit issue, things become much more complicated as pointed out by Rauch (1991). Accordingly to him, per-unit-distance transportation costs within the country always account for the final node of volume of trade than the same exportable items of other countries. These costs combined with the assumption that cities are the basic units of spatial organisation in a country lead the model to predict that population size, wage rates, and residential rental rates of cities will all decline monotonically as one moves inland from a coastal port. But casual empiricism suggests that such theorisation is only an exception rather than a rule in present Indian situation of human settlement and concentration of industries. There is also a belief that transport is a safe investment politically. Hirschman (1958) suggests that perhaps it is the absence of criteria and of sanctions that endears transportation investments so much to developers.

We have so far seen that some studies have addressed the role of transport in regional development but very few of them have assessed the significance of ports therein. There is also no dearth of studies that have focused on regional disparity in India in general during the last few decades, but not a single study has taken port facility as an infrastructure attribute to assess either regional disparity or trade impediment in India.[9]

A port grows by virtue of the trade it can attract. Its growth is a function not only of technologically related supply facilities but also of the economic and political objectives of a country that determine the demand for port services. The history of port development is often an

9 However, some recent studies have dealt with the infrastructure facilities and income in general. For example, Elhance and Lakshmanan (1988), Binswanger, Khandkur and Rosenwing (1989), Ghosh and De (1998, 2000a, 2004, 2005a, 2005b).

epitome of changing economic, political and technological circumstances on various scales aided by outward orientation of the economy (Ray, 1993; Kindleberger, 1996). An efficient port raises the productivity of other factors of production (labour and capital) and profitability of the producing units thereby permitting higher levels of output, income and/or employment.

During the last few decades the increased globalisation and intensified competition in world trade have been resulted not only from the liberalisation of trade policies but also from significant advances in transport, communication, storage and power facilities. These developments have transformed the traditional organisation of production and marketing in order to gain in competitive advantage in the international market. The main focus here is on the management and transport logistics to achieve efficient utilisation of inputs thereby permitting rapid response to emerging facilities, and to cripple the abilities of even the resourceful countries to emerge as major players in the global market. In India, some worthy and unheeded works have started to come out which deal explicitly with non-price factors as the most important barriers to India's success in foreign trade (Peters, 1990; EXIM Bank, 1998; De, 2009b, 2009c). Thus, beyond the price factors which fail to pay any heed to the role of supply side factors relating to infrastructure, the ability of the developing countries to provide the required transport and communication services essential for modern logistics management will increasingly determine their ability to compete for export market and direct foreign investments. Mexico's maquiladora operations, Chile's exports of fruits, Columbia's of cut flowers and Kenya's of horticultural products are examples where countries have been able to meet logistical requirements of their overseas customers. On the other hand, there are many examples of countries which are loosing the competitive edge because of shortcomings both in key infrastructure as well as in institutional and procedural delays, especially relating to custom processing and transport services. In India, the freight rates of container traffic and transit times through ports exceed those of her Asian competitors by large margins (De, 2005). This seriously constrains India's export promotion goals. Therefore, the success of on-going economic reforms, which is essentially a sort of export-led growth strategy, crucially hinges on the level, development and utilisation of transport and communication infrastructure, especially port.

1.4 Overview of Indian Ports: Pre-Independence Period

The ancient Indian ports were well equipped to hold, harbour and handle the wooden ships of those days. Indians excelled in manufacturing these ships. The oldest wooden warship, HMS Foudroyant – formerly Trincomalee – now berthed at Portsmouth, was built by the Wadias in 1817 (Sahai, 1996). The flagship Asia of Admiral Codrington used in the Battle of Navarino was made at the Nawroji Cursetji yard in 1824 (Sahai, 1996). But with the advent of steel-and-steam huge ships of thousands of tones, the entire complexion of seaborne trade and the port facilities required was changed. The ports had to be planned *de novo* to meet the requirements of modern ships. It was, fortunately, around this tie that India launched her own industrial revolution.

The story of organised industry in India may be said to have begun when Framji Banaji started the first spinning and weaving mill at Bombay in 1845. The first steam cotton-spinning factory was opened by Cowasjee Davar, also at Bombay, in 1854 (Sahai, 1996). The foundation of jute mills was laid a year later near Calcutta (now called Kolkata), mostly with foreign capital and enterprise. The opening of the first railway line in April 1853 which chugged its way from Bombay to Thane revolutionised internal transport. It was extended up to Kassarah in 1861, to Nagpur in 1867 and to Jabalpur in 1870. The line from Bombay to Ahmedabad was built in 1864 and by 1871, though rail communications from the port towns of Calcutta and Madras were completed.

Simultaneously, the telegraph system was opened in 1858 and by 1860 the port town of Bombay, Calcutta and Madras were linked by telegraph system to various ports of the country. Four years later, in 1864, cables were laid between India and Europe via Turkey, and in

1870, via Aden and Suez. These developments constituted an industrial revolution in India of sort, which boosted industry, and ports had to be remodelled to take on increased traffic.

Records reveal that as late as in 1870, the port of Bombay, though the best then, was merely a shallow harbour without any built-in dock to hold deep drafted vessels. It did not have adequate shore equipment to handle cargo. Even when the first dock, the Sassoon Dock, was built in 1875, it could not hold more than five 1000-tonne vessels at a time. Calcutta port had only screw pile jetties with some steam cranes and sheds. The port of Cochin, a good harbour, could receive only vessels up to three metre draft; the bigger vessels had to wait in the outer sea and their cargo was brought to shore on small country boats. The situation at Madras and Visakhapatnam ports was worse since both were roadstead and not harbours. All the vessels visiting those ports were anchored in the outer sea. Even the best harbours then were just good enough to take low drafted carrying 100–200 tonnes of cargo.

In the decade ending 1850, no steamers visited the Bombay port and the average size of the sailing ships was only 450 GRT in foreign trade and around 200 GRT in the coastal trade. During the 1850s, on an average, 36 steamers sailed in Bombay annually and their average size was around 900 tonnes. But between 1901 and 1906, 641 steamers visited the port and their average size shot up to 2,360 registered tonnes. This compelled the port authorities to provide facilities for accommodating bigger vessels requiring deeper draft. With the opening of the Suez Canal in 1869, the ocean distance between India and Europe was drastically reduced which gave a fillip to trade and imparted urgency to port development schemes (Sahai, 1986).

It was between 1870 and 1915 that the task of port development was taken up in right earnest. Whereas the first dock in London Port was opened in 1700, and at Liverpool in 1715, in India the work was taken up 150 years later. What encouraged this activity was the opening of Suez Canal, beginning of organised manufacturing industry, development of transport services and the introduction of large-size steamships. All the major docks at Bombay, Calcutta and Madras were constructed during these 50 years. The ports of Cochin, Karachi, and Mormugao were also developed during this period.

At Cochin, modern port facilities were initiated in 1870, at Karachi, the construction of breakwaters was completed in 1887; and the Mormugao port with its breakwaters and berths as also its railway connections, was completed in 1888. At Bombay, the Prince's Dock with 10 berths and 6 metre draft was completed in 1880, the Victoria Dock with 13 berths and 7½ metre draft in 1888, and the Alexandria Dock with 20 berths and 9½ metre draft in 1914. In Calcutta, the Kidderpore Dock was built in 1893 and in Madras, its artificial arm, an enclosed basin, was constructed during 1910–16. Gradually, as infrastructural facilities were created and an industrial base built, old ports were developed and fresh ones set up.

In the pre-independence period, two additional coastal towns were developed as modern ports. These were Cochin and Visakhapatnam. Cochin, a natural harbour, had been a renowned commercial centre successively under the Portuguese, the Dutch and the English. It was sought to be developed into a major port as early as the 1880s, but it was not until the 1920s that the project was taken in hand. The port was opened to ocean going vessels around 1930, the first two shore berths along with concomitant facilities were provided in 1940 and two additional shore berths added soon after. It was during this period that Visakhapatnam was also developed to provide shipping facilities over the long coastlines stretching between Calcutta and Madras. The elopement work started in right earnest in 1925, and by 1933 the port was open for traffic.

1.5 Development of Ports: Post-Independence Period

At present, India is endowed with an extensive coastline along nine coastal states. These states are Gujarat, Maharashtra, Karnataka, Goa, Kerala (west coast) and Tamil Nadu, Andhra Pradesh, Orissa, West Bengal (east coast). These nine states have in total 13 major and 187 non-major (previously known as minor) ports (Government of India, 2007). Among these 13 major ports, six are located in the west coast (Kandla, Mumbai, Jawaharlal Nehru, Mormugao, Cochin, and New Mangalore) and seven in the east coast (Ennore, Chennai, Tuticorin, Paradip, Vizag, Kolkata, and Haldia). Out of 187 non-major ports, 125 ports belong to west coast comprising 67 percent of total Indian non-major ports, 27 ports belong to east coast and the rest, 35 belong to Union Territories.[10] Maharashtra has the highest number of ports – two major and 53 non-major. Next to it is Gujarat, where one major and 40 non-major ports are situated.

However, at Independence, India was left with five major ports, namely, Bombay, Calcutta, Madras, Cochin and Visakhapatnam. With the loss of Karachi to Pakistan, the need was felt to have an alternative port as also to provide another deep draft port between Bombay and Cochin. A committee was set up to examine the locations of new ports. The Kasturbhai Lalbhai Committee recommended Malpe near Mangalore and Kandla as the two sites. A subsequent committee, the Intermediate Port Development Committee, however shifted the location from Malpe to Mangalore. The construction of Kandla port was also recommended in 1948 by the West Coast Major Port Development Committee (Sahai, 1986).[11]

Work on Kandla started in 1949 and it became the sixth major port in 1955. It serves as the gateway for the entire hinterland comprising the whole of Rajasthan, Punjab, and Jammu & Kashmir for international trade and commerce. Surprisingly, even the state of Assam at the eastern extreme serves as a hinterland to Kandla because the transport of export tea and jute over the meter gauge in quite competitive compared to export through the Calcutta port. Mormugao, developed by the Portuguese long ago, was declared as a major port after its liberation, in

10 Due to the lack of overseas cargo, some maritime states like Andhra Pradesh and Kerala closed down few minor ports which are called non-working ports.

11 All the four Committees, appointed by the Government of India during 1942–1948, found Mangalore as the best port site (Sahai, 1986).

1963. Paradip in the East coast came up in 1966. New Mangalore took a long time to materialise and joined as a major port in 1974 along with Tuticorin. Nhava Sheva established in 1989, whereas Ennore was in 2003. Thus, the country today has 13 major ports: Bombay set up in

Figure 1.1 Location of Ports on Indian Coast

Source: Ministry of Shipping, Road Transport, and Highways, Government of India

1875, Calcutta (1893), Madras (1916), Vizag (1933), Mormugao (1963), Cochin (1870), Paradip (1966), Haldia (1965), Kandla (1955), New Mangalore and Tuticorin (both in 1974), Nhava Sheva (1989), and Ennore (2003). Locations of these ports are plotted in Figure 1.1.

1.6 Institutional Set-up

Ports in India are classified as 'Major Ports' and 'Non-major (minor) Ports'. Major ports come under the jurisdiction of the Central government and by virtue of entry 27 in the List I of Schedule VII of the Constitution of India, form part of the Central subject. The Major Port Trusts Act, 1963 and the Indian Ports Act, 1908, basically govern them. Ports other than Major ports are included among the subject of the List III (concurrent list – entry 31), and hence are controlled and operated by state governments subject to certain central legislation being operative on them as well. The primary responsibility for the development and management of minor and intermediate ports rests with the state governments within the purview of Indian Ports Act, 1908 (Figure 1.2).

The Indian Ports Act, 1908 describes the regulatory powers of the port authority whereas the Major Port Trusts Act, 1963 enables the ports to conduct its regulatory as well as commercial functions. The Indian Ports Act, 1908 applies automatically to all ports and parts of navigable rivers and channels leading to the ports, irrespective of category, i.e. major and non-major. The Major Port Trusts Act, 1963 is restricted to the port proper of the major ports.

Therefore, 'Major Ports' may be any ports which the Central government may, by notification in the Central Gazette, declare under the Indian Ports Act, 1908, or may under any law for the time being in force have declared to be a major port.[12] 'Other Port' means any port, which the state governments may, by notification in state gazette, declare as a minor port.

Major Port Trusts Act, 1963 empowers the Central government to constitute a Board of Trustees for each major port. The planning of major ports is done by the Ministry of Shipping, Road Transport, and

12 Ports of Calcutta, Bombay and Madras were declared as 'Major Port', pursuant statutory enactment dated 16. 12. 1920, and were brought under the direct control of the Central Government by virtue of the Seventh Schedule of the Government of India Act, 1935.

Highways, Government of India on the basis of plans drawn up by port trusts and in consultation with other organisations like the Planning Commission, National Development Council, Ministry of Commerce and Industry, Ministry of Finance, etc.

The nature and scope of the regulatory environment in the Indian port sector is derived from a number of existing shipping and port-related laws. The port laws have been enacted to address specific areas relating to shipping and port operations and enforced through various statutory agencies under the executive authority of Central and State governments. The laws currently in force which have a bearing on port operations can be broadly grouped into (i) port laws, (ii) port labour laws, (iii) shipping laws, and (iv) environment-related laws.

In general, maritime administration in India is governed by five acts, namely, (i) Indian Ports Act, 1908, (ii) Major Port Trust Act, 1963, (iii) Dock Workers (Regulation of Employment) Act, 1948, (iv) Dock Workers (Safety, Health & Welfare) Act, 1986, and (v) The Merchant Shipping Act, 1958. There are other general enactments that have a bearing on port like the Industrial Disputes Act, 1947 and Customs Act, 1962. The Environment (Protection) Act, 1986 and the rules / regulations framed there under are relevant to port development and operations. In India, the Tariff Authority of Major Ports (TAMP), constituted in 1997, is an independent authority and is the sole regulator of Indian major ports to regulate and notify all tariffs.

1.7 Profile of Indian Ports

Ports are prime infrastructure outlets contributing to the growth of world economies. The phenomenal rise in world trade in recent decades is linked to the increasing integration of national economies across the world. Rapid global advancements in information and communication technologies allow collaboration on industries and trade throughout the world and increases output at competitive costs resulting in a boom in

Table 1.2 Cargo Handled by Major Ports of India, 2007–08

	POL[1]	Iron Ore	Fertilizer		Coal		Container		Other Cargo[2]	Total
			Finished	Raw Materials	Thermal	Coking	Tonnage	Number		
	Million Tonnes							M.TEUs	Million Tonnes	
Kolkata	4.52	0.49		0.03			5.14	0.30	3.57	13.74
Haldia	17.84	9.82	0.36	0.35	1.80	5.46	2.24	0.13	5.67	43.54
Paradip	1.75	12.96	0.14	3.42	13.35	4.73	0.05	0.00	6.04	42.44
Visakhapatnam (Vizag)	19.81	18.69	3.28	0.72	2.90	7.49	1.13	0.07	10.59	64.60
Ennore	0.32	2.19			9.05				0.00	11.56
Chennai	12.79	10.82	0.62	0.27	2.33	1.66	18.05	1.02	10.62	57.15
Tuticorin	0.46		1.10	0.63	6.11		5.63	0.45	7.55	21.48
Cochin	11.30		0.08	0.27	0.25		3.24	0.25	0.67	15.81
New Mangalore	21.78	9.27	0.83	0.01		1.69	0.32	0.02	2.12	36.02
Mormugao	0.87	27.33	0.19		0.36	3.89	0.14	0.01	2.35	35.13
Mumbai	37.07		0.10	0.21	2.95		1.63	0.12	15.07	57.04
Jawaharlal Nehru	2.24						51.84	4.06	1.67	55.76
Kandla	38.18	0.42	3.92	0.16	0.94	0.24	2.64	0.16	18.40	64.89
All Major Ports	168.94	91.97	10.61	6.07	40.03	25.16	92.05	6.60	84.33	519.16

Notes: 1.Petroleum, Oil and Lubricants. 2. Miscellaneous cargoes. 3. An empty cell means cargo not handled by the respective port 4. M.TEUs means Million TEUs.

Source: Indian Ports Association, New Delhi

Figure 1.2 Indian Port Sector: Institutional Framework

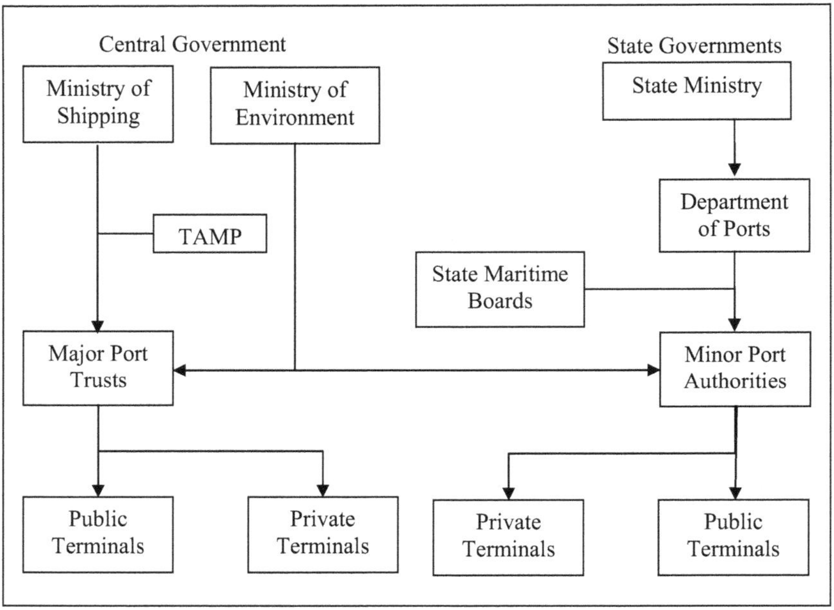

world trade. This booming global trade has led to the increased importance and rapid development of ports and container terminals geared for fast and efficient movement of cargo.

A considerably high portion of the total Indian seaborne traffic (71 percent in 2006–07) is handled by major ports of India. With an average annual growth rate of 10 percent, the total traffic handled by the major ports of India has increased from 156.64 million tonnes in 1991–92 to 463.78 million tonnes in 2006–07. Kandla, Vizag, and Chennai are the top three largest major ports, which in together share 36 percent of the Indian major port traffic in 2007–08 (Table 1.2). Table 1.2 shows that, except Ennore, which is a new port dedicated to handle coal and iron ore, rest of the Indian major ports handle a diverse varieties cargo. Haldia, Vizag, New Mangalore and Kandla can be termed as India's bulk cargo handling ports, whereas Jawaharlal Nehru, which is South Asia's largest container port, exclusively handling containerised cargo.

India being an energy deficient country imports more than 60 percent of petroleum, oil and lubricants (POL) every year, resulting which, most of its ports (except Ennore) handle POL traffic. In 2007–08, 13 major Indian ports handled 169 million tonnes of POL traffic, up from 154 million tonnes of 2006–07. Similarly, India is one of the largest exporters of coal in the world, which results in the rest of the ports handling large volumes of coal traffic. In fact, the new port, Ennore, only handles domestic and international trade in coal and iron ore.

Containerisation started in India in 1973 in a limited way with the creation of interim container handling facilities at Mumbai and Chennai ports. Since then container traffic has steadily increased over the years. Container traffic has been recording an impressive 50 percent per annum growth particularly since 1990–91, in accordance with the increasing containerisation of general cargoes for international trade. At present, the country is handling approximately 6.60 million TEUs of container

Figure 1.3 Container Traffic Handled by Major Ports of India

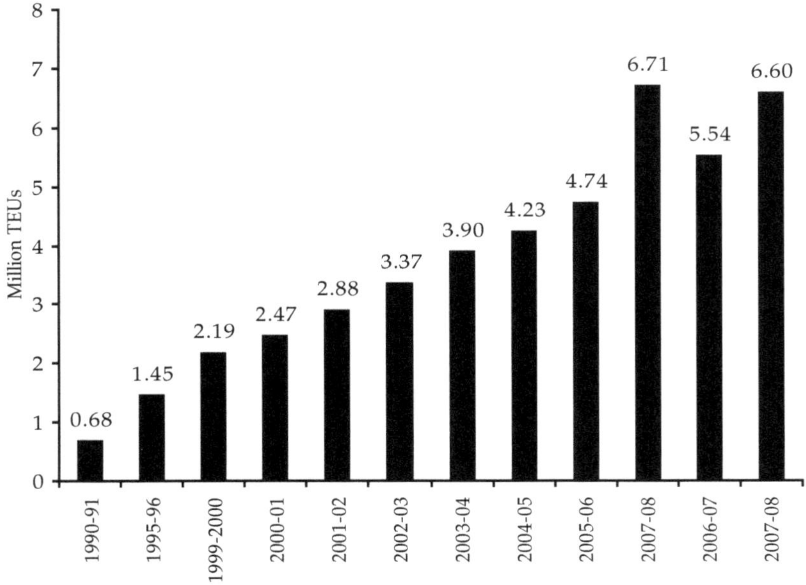

Source: Indian Ports Association, New Delhi

Figure 1.4 Indian Container Ports and Their Shares in 2007–08

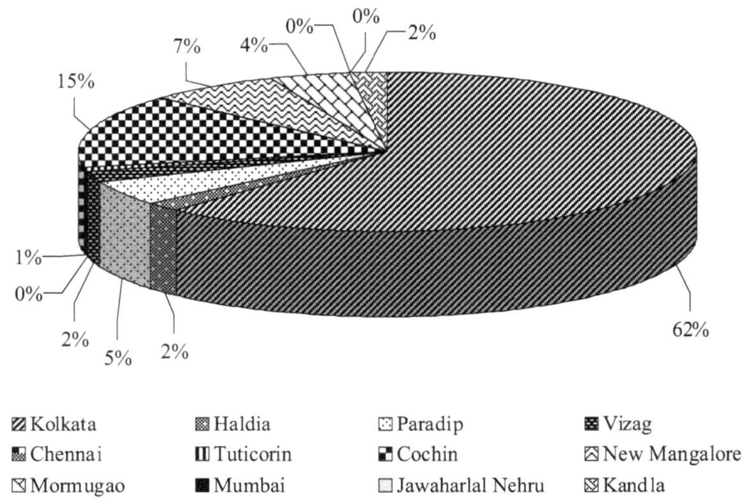

Source: Indian Ports Association, New Delhi

Figure 1.5 Growth Matrix of Indian Container Ports

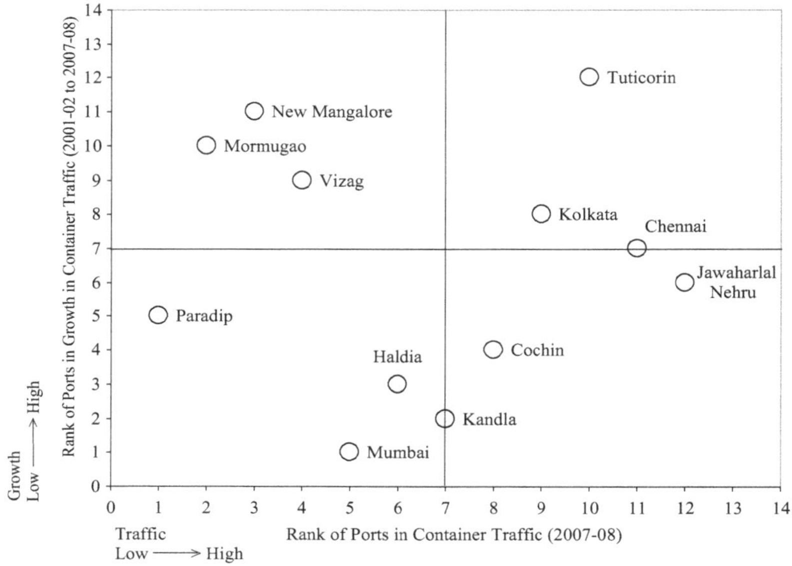

Table 1.3 Maritime State-wise Port Traffic in 2006–07

States	Major Ports		Non-Major Ports		Total		Share in Total Cargo (%)
	Number	Cargo (Million Tonnes)	Number	Cargo (Million Tonnes)	Number	Cargo (Million Tonnes)	
Gujarat	1	52.98	40	132.44	41	185.42	28.54
Maharashtra	2	97.18	53	11.56	55	108.74	16.74
Goa	1	34.24	7*	14.31	8	48.55	7.47
Karnataka	1	32.04	10	6.56	11	38.60	5.94
Kerala	1	15.26	13	0.08	14	15.34	2.36
Tamil Nadu	3	82.13	15	0.71	18	82.84	12.75
Andhra Pradesh	1	56.39	12	18.61	13	75.00	11.54
Orissa	1	38.52	2	0.05	3	38.57	5.94
West Bengal	2	55.05	1		3	55.05	8.47
Others**			34	1.60	34	1.60	0.25
Total	13	463.78	187	185.87	200	649.70	100.00

Notes: *Including Non-Major ports located in Daman and Diu. **Ports located in Pondicherry, Andaman and Nicobar Islands and Lakshadweep.

Source: Ministry of Shipping, Road Transport, and Highways, Government of India

Table 1.4 Average Annual Growth Rate of Port Traffic

(%)

Port	1993–94 to 2003–04			2003–04			2004–05		
	Int.	Dom.	Total	Int.	Dom.	Total	Int.	Dom.	Total
Major Ports	7.17	5.68	6.77	13.83	–0.22	9.97	14.23	2.48	11.30
Non-Major Ports	19.94	19.54	19.83	12.20	3.43	9.75	19.92	2.11	15.23
All Ports	9.19	7.92	8.85	13.41	0.73	9.91	15.67	2.38	12.31

Notes: Int.: International (Overseas) Traffic. Dom.: Domestic (Coastal) Traffic
Source: Ministry of Shipping, Government of India

(Figure 1.3). Jawaharlal Nehru port alone shares 62 percent (4.06 million TEUs) of total Indian container traffic (Figure 1.4). Next to it is Chennai, which shares 15 percent (1.02 million TEUs). With the exception of Ennore, the rest of 12 major ports have started handling containers, but not all are running in optimum potential. For instance, Tuticorin, Kolkata and Chennai can be termed as India's top three potential ports which are placed in the 'High Growth – High Traffic' category. See the upper right box in the Figure 1.5. Jawaharlal Nehru port, located in India's western coast, is India's largest container port. These four ports are seemingly in a league of their own, in relation to the others. These are the ports on which India applied its first generation port reforms in the 1990s, starting with leasing out container terminals to P&O Ports (now known as DP World), namely, NSICT (Jawaharlal Nehru) in 1997 and CCT (Chennai) in 2001, and to Port of Singapore Authority (PSA) (Tuticorin) in 1999.

Except Ennore and Jawaharlal Nehru ports, the rest of India's major ports were developed between 40 and 140 years ago. Nurturing these old ports with reform packages in tandem with on-going global development processes is not an easy task, especially when most of these ports are overburdened with surplus labour and obsolete technology. Therefore, adding new capacities along the lines of existing facilities in every major port is chosen as popular way to redefine the destiny of the Indian port sector.

Major and non-major ports in India collectively handled 650 million tonnes of cargo in 2006–07, of which major ports handled 464 million tonnes and non-major ports handled 186 million tonnes (Table 1.3). The growth in cargo has been phenomenal in non-major ports, where cargo increased by about 20 percent in non-major ports, almost three times that of major ports in the post-liberalisation period (1993–94 to 2003–04) (Table 1.4). Non-major ports thus have been emerging as serious contenders to the major ports for a share in the sea-borne cargo, both international and domestic cargo.

With respect to the contribution of the individual maritime states to the total cargo traffic handled by all the ports in 2006–07 (Table 1.3), it was observed that Gujarat with 28.54 percent comes first among the maritime states. With 16.74 and 12.75 percent share, Maharashtra and Tamil Nadu come next. Gujarat is the only state, which has been witnessing increase in its share of sea-borne cargo in total traffic over the years; its share has increased from 17.63 percent during 1990–91 to 28.54 percent in 2006–07 due to the development of several non-major ports in the state with the active participation of the private sector and local government. Today, two of India's most successful non-major seaports are Mundra and Pipavav, both located in Gujarat.

Impact of Performance Indicators and Labour Endowment on Port Traffic

2.1 Introduction

Having discussed the profile of Indian ports, our purpose in this chapter is to find out the relationship between port performance, labour endowment and port traffic in Indian port sector.

Since the deregulation of the US domestic transport sector, the transport industries across the world have witnessed major reorganisation (Simon, 1996).[1] In the subsequent period, the port sector in many developing countries has been undergoing transformation from a subsistence infrastructure resource into a more capital intensive, commercially oriented facility. More than US$ 8 billion of private capital has been pledged for capacity expansion and service modernisation in Far Eastern and Southeastern Asian ports (Peters, 1995). Ports in the United States have invested about US$ 20 billion over the last 25 years; of this, US$ 12 billion has been invested just between 1997–2006 in channel deepening and infrastructure projects (Tamaki, 1999; Haveman, 2007). This description represents a process initiated in the nineties which saw many of the ports across the world to undertake major policy changes in order to increase port productivity. Interestingly, this structural transformation has coincided with significant increases in countries' exports.

1 However, empirical studies of the transport industry have provided little evidence of the presence of scale economies. Specialised research works in this field have been made by Keeler (1974, 1983) on railways, Caves, Christensen and Tretheway (1984), Bauer (1990), Khumbhakar (1992) on airlines, McMullen (1987), Winston, Corsi, Grimm and Evans (1990) on trucking industries, and Coto-Millan et al. (2000), Notteboom et al. (2000) on ports.

In India, interest in the effect of public capital on port infrastructure has increased in recent years partly as a result of numerous reports regarding the fragile state of the country's infrastructure. To sustain 9 percent growth, the Government of India has estimated that an investment of over US$ 492.5 billion is required in the infrastructure sector in India during the 11th Five Year Plan (2007–2012), of which port sector needs US$ 18 billion (Government of India, 2007). The importance of public capital for the growth of the port sector stems from the chain linkage between production, performance of individual ports and overseas transportation leading to exports.[2]

Traditionally, by virtue of various legal stipulations, government controls national ports in many developing countries. However, rising inefficiencies in ports have forced the governments to deregulate the system (Kuby and Reid, 1992; Estache and Carbajo, 1997; Bollard and Pickford, 1998). The effects of poor port performance on a country's trade have become too obvious (Juhel, 1999). Inefficient ports, whether through lack of integrated transport network, outdated work practices or obsolete facilities, can stall a country's growth even in a borderless world. The unreliability and poor quality of infrastructural services often add to the costs of production of exportable and adversely affect a country's international competitiveness (De, 2008b; Srinivasan, 2000). The present study addresses these issues in the context of India. There are some studies, which have tried to understand the relation between a country's openness and port performance, but few have touched upon the empirical causality between port performance and port traffic. Al-

2 Public capital in port sector such as radio wireless station, pilot vessels, mooring boats, tugs, cranes and trailers of various types, warehousing and storage facilities, water supply and energy facilities, fire fighting utilities, conservancy, etc. could be viewed as inputs in the service process which contribute independently to the cargo handling. Under the present institutional set up, the role of private capital in Indian ports is very limited. Yet, it is generally taken for granted that decades of 'sheltered market' phenomenon has not created among Indian industrialists any 'outward looking' tendency. Moreover, high 'gestation lag' in the port sector is believed to be the main cause for low level of private capital in this sector even under the selective liberalisation initiated by the Government in the post-1991 period.

ternative views about the causal relationship between these variables of economic interest exist. Economic theory provides no firm basis to judge whether performance causes traffic or traffic causes performance. There may be a latent simultaneity between the two, given the overall economic perspective of a country.

The organisation of the chapter is as follows. Section 2.2 deals with data and methodology. Individual performance of Indian ports, along with the construction of a port performance index (PPI) with the help of principal component analysis, is discussed in Section 2.3. Section 2.4 tests the impact of port performance and labour endowment on port traffic. Policy implications are discussed in Section 2.5. Finally, concluding remarks are briefed in Section 2.6.

2.2 Data and Methodology

The major exploit of this chapter is port facility. In general, port facility can be taken as public infrastructure input from the supply side. Here, we have taken eight important variables for 12 major ports for four different time points over the period from 1985 to 2005, to judge relative port performance. These include (i) ship turn-round time (TRT), (ii) pre-berthing waiting time (PBWT), (iii) percentage of idle time at berth to time at working berth (PITTWB), (iv) output per ship berth day (OSBD), (v) berth throughput rate (BTR), (vi) berth occupancy rate (BOR), (vii) operating surplus per ton of cargo handled (PTOS) and (viii) rate of return on turnover (RRT).

The functional values of the port performance indicators appear to give a fairly representative and reasonable picture of port efficiency. Application of traditional production function methodology to spatial production units like airports and seaports, in order to find out the nature and strength of the explanatory variables, is not new, particularly when the sole independent variables are labour and capital. But beyond the conventional wisdom in production economics, ports unlike other manufacturing decision making units (DMU), represent a spatial production system which can not be fully understood simply by the quantity of labour and capital alone even under equal demand conditions. One must probe deeper into the natural geo-navigational settings in which a port is situated. The adversity or favourability of the inherent locational features of a port ultimately dictate the desired amount of capital expenditures which significantly affect the efficiency of operation at various layers of management, not necessarily all in the port complex. Hence, port performance efficiency is expected to be highly contingent upon the indicators listed above. Thus, the mere amount of capital is not sufficient. What is important is how this capital is allocated and utilised in order to enhance port performance. Ideally, Y = f (L, K). But in the case of a spatial DMU like a port, the optimal combination of geo-navigational and strategic factors, along with current labour, are ultimately responsible for port performance rather than the mere amount of capital.

In any developing country like India, the problem lies in the fact that a very large proportion of public sector allocation is diluted through the political bureaucracy nexus (Bardhan and Mukherjee, 1998; Marjit, 1999), and the efficiency of utilisation of public capital significantly varies across regions (Ghosh, Marjit and Neogi, 1998). Thus, there is reasonable consensus among the economists that the mobility of goods, services and labour across the regions depends largely on the quality and quantity of various integrated facilities available, and not directly on the amount taxpayers pay or posterity will have to. Naturally therefore, the port performance indicators are likely to better reflect the input output relationship relative to capital in such a context. The point is not that capital is unimportant. Had there been complete information on capital accumulation and some quantitative idea on public corruption at various layers of fund disbursement and execution across each region, it would have been justified to work with capital stock pertaining to the relevant infrastructures for measuring the performance of the ports. Thus, we propose to use Y = f (L, PPI), although for the purpose of verification we shall include capital as a third independent variable thereby making the production function as follows.

$$Y = f(L, PPI, K) \qquad (2.1)$$

The details of PPI and its construction are explained in Section 2.3.2. Labour endowment is represented by the total number of labourers employed in each port. Following Nijkamp (1984), one could use activity rate of labourers, i.e., share of each port's labourers to total Indian port labourers. However, in our case, the specific form of the production function is as follows.

$$Y_i = f(L_i^{\alpha}, PPI_i^{\beta}, K_i^{\gamma}) \qquad (2.2)$$

Taking log of equation (2.2) and adding a dummy, we get

$$Ln(Y_i) = a + \alpha\, Ln(L_i) + \beta\, Ln(PPI_i) + \gamma\, Ln(K_i) + \phi\, D \qquad (2.3)$$

where Y = traffic of individual port, L = labour, PPI = weighted port performance index, K = capital, i represents individual port (i=1,...,12), and D represents time dummy with D=1 for later year and D=0 for other in two different pair of years, namely, 1985–86 and 2005–06, and 1991–92 and 2005–06. The time dummy will help us understand the role of natural rate of growth in terms of a shift effected over a time span.

From equation (2.3), the impact of PPI and labour on traffic can be estimated in this comparative static framework. In the case of a positive association between the independent and dependent variables, the values of α, β, γ and ϕ should be greater than zero. Here, α, β and γ represent the elasticity of traffic with respect to labour, port performance and capital respectively. If time as an independent variable positively influences port traffic, then ϕ must be greater than zero too. Negative values of α, β, γ and ϕ imply opposite results.

This function has been estimated for two different pair of time points, 1985–86 and 2005–06, and 1991–92 and 2005–06 for 12 major ports in a cross section time-series pooled data set.[3] The choice of the initial year (1985–86) is influenced by the fact that since the mid-80s, India embarked for the first time upon a path of trade

3 These ports are Kandla, Mumbai, Jawaharlal Nehru, Mormugao, Cochin, New Mangalore, Ennore, Chennai, Tuticorin, Paradip, Vizag, and Kolkata. Haldia port being an administrative part of Kolkata Port Trust, in this paper, Kolkata port represents both Kolkata and Haldia docks.

liberalisation with special emphasis on the electronics sector. In 1991–92, India undertook economic reform as explicit state policy which began with the announcement of the new Industrial Policy in July, 1991. A break at 1991–92 helps evaluate the nature of the relationship among the variables in the post-liberalisation period.[4] Due to the lack of adequate information on performance indicators, minor ports have not been considered in this study.

The main data for this study have been collected from various issues of (i) Basic Ports Statistics of India, and (ii) Transport Statistics of India - all published by the Ministry of Shipping, Road Transport and Highways, Government of India. This data set is supplemented by several issues of 'Major Ports of India: A Profile', published by the Indian Ports Association, New Delhi.

2.2.1 Measures of Performance

We attempt to measure the performance of Indian major ports by developing a composite index, called port performance index (PPI) comprising indicators of operational performance (TRT, PBWT), asset performance (OSBD, BTR, BOR) and financial performance (PTOS, RRT).[5] We have taken eight individual variables, as described

4 India followed the strategy of planning ever since the First Five Year Plan (1951–56). 1991 (July) marks the beginning of the era of market economy away from centralised planning. The new economic policy became effective from this year. The salient features of this policy, to start with, were as follows: (i) To allow direct foreign capital in industries, trading companies and banking up to 51 percent of share capital (in some cases, 100 percent); (ii) Automatic clearance for capital goods import; (iii) Automatic approval of foreign technology agreements in high priority areas; (iv) setting up of Foreign Investment Promotion Board for negotiating with MNCs and granting single point clearance; (v) Permission of private sector banking; (vi) Other measures include the abolition of industrial licensing except limited areas, abolition of MRTP and FERA, closing down of chronically sick public sector units etc. Sadly enough, no major fundamental policy change pertaining to port sector could be visualised in 1991.

in Section 2.2, of the major ports, for three different time points, over the period from 1985–86 to 2005–06. The definitions of the performance indicators are briefed in Appendix 2.1. The basic limitation of the conventional method of constructing a composite index from a number of indicators is that often subjective and fixed weights are given to individual indicators, which actually vary over time and space. To overcome this limitation, we employ the well-known multivariate technique of 'factor analysis' (or what is known as 'principal component analysis') (PCA) from which the weights of the respective factors follow (Fruchter, 1967).

In the PCA approach, the first principal component is a linear combination of the weighted variables which explains the maximum of variance across space. Hence, here, the sole objective of the weighting mechanism is to explain the maximum variance for all the individual indicators across the ports at a point in time. The rationale for using principal component analysis is that it helps one to reach an aggregative representation from various individual port performance indicators. Its broader objective is quite pari pasu with homogenising the overall requirements for the individual indicators across the ports.

2.2.2 Construction of PPI

We have at our disposal values of eight port performance variables for three different years, 1985–86, 1991–92, and 2005–06, across 12 major ports. The details of the factor loadings (weights) derived from the PCA of these performance variables are presented in Table 2.1(a) and the estimated PPI in Table 2.1(b). PPI is a linear combination of the unit free values of the individual indicators such that

$$PPI_{ij} = \Sigma W_{kj} X_{kij} \qquad (2.4)$$

5 For a critical and comprehensive review of the methods for measuring performance of a port system, one may consult Chung (1993), Frankel (1987), Fourgeard (1999), Plumlee (1982), and UNCTAD (1983, 1987).

where PPI_{ij} = port performance index of the ith port in j^{th} time, W_{kj} = weight of kth indicator in j^{th} time, and X_{kij} = unit free value of the kth indicator for the ith port in j^{th} time. Each individual indicator was made unit free dividing by the standard deviation across the ports. A few observations are worth noting here.

First, we have not found a single variable that has emerged as the most influential factor in all the years. The variables which have emerged as influential determining factors before 1991 come out as less important factors in the post-liberalisation period. However, looking at the overall consecutive good rankings of TRT, BTR and PBWT during the period, it is felt that these variables have played influential role in determining the performance of individual ports.

Second, PBWT, BOR, TRT and BTR have been found to be important determinants of performance in the post-liberalisation period during 1991–92 to 2005–06. Thus, two each of the operational performance indicators (TRT and PBWT) and asset performance indicators (BTR, BOR) have emerged as decisive factors in determining the PPI in the post-liberalisation period.

Third, in the post-liberalisation period, India has witnessed a rise in her overseas trade volumes. A substantial part of this overseas trade has passed through the ports, and this is directly reflected in the port capacity utilisation rate. During the period from 1991–92 to 2005–06, Indian ports have been over-utilised. Port congestion is quite likely to prevail in the coming years, if this rate of progression continues. Broadly speaking, when there is high congestion at a port, performance is influenced by coordination among different processes as well as the speed of clearance of vessels from the berth. In the short run when capacity is over-utilised, coordination among various intra-port outfits and speed of clearance of vessels are the only ways out for tackling congestion. As a matter of fact, this has been reflected in the year 2005–06 when two of our operational performance indicators (PBWT and TRT), and one asset performance indicator (BOR) became the first three important factors in terms of weights in determining performance of an individual port.

Fourth, unlike popular belief, financial performance indicators like PTOS and RRI have emerged as factors of low importance in determin-

Table 2.1(a). Weights of Port Performance Indicators

Year	TRT	PBWT	PITTWB	OSBD	BOR	BTR	PTOS	RRT	Eigen Value[1]	EV[2]
1985–86	–0.539	0.417	–0.604	0.876	0.580	0.636	0.803	0.893	3.782	0.533
1986–87	–0.503	0.381	–0.683	0.950	0.271	0.658	0.077	0.383	2.425	0.403
1987–88	–0.781	–0.110	–0.520	0.873	–0.260	0.696	0.408	0.682	2.839	0.455
1988–89	0.584	0.906	0.054	0.142	0.867	0.651	–0.281	0.756	3.010	0.496
1989–90	–0.329	–0.396	0.603	0.701	0.432	0.763	0.401	0.629	2.445	0.406
1990–91	–0.393	–0.074	0.299	0.824	0.160	0.881	–0.690	0.625	2.597	0.425
1991–92	–0.171	0.514	–0.507	0.763	0.671	0.766	–0.636	0.299	2.663	0.433
1992–93	0.128	0.834	–0.419	0.806	0.849	0.762	–0.511	0.462	3.312	0.504
1993–94	0.130	0.780	–0.695	0.673	0.768	0.576	–0.514	0.731	3.282	0.510
1994–95	0.672	0.767	–0.741	–0.065	0.811	0.208	0.348	0.870	3.173	0.497
1995–96	0.877	0.853	–0.899	0.194	0.729	0.539	0.109	0.619	3.559	0.515
1996–97	0.728	0.912	–0.686	0.033	0.822	0.457	–0.458	0.154	2.950	0.439
1997–98	0.615	0.794	–0.241	0.654	0.790	0.680	–0.689	–0.050	3.061	0.493
1998–99	0.782	0.892	0.138	0.248	0.891	0.446	–0.520	0.283	2.831	0.422
1999–00	0.772	0.870	0.139	0.241	0.892	0.454	0.120	0.261	2.988	0.456
2000–01	0.753	0.939	0.144	0.243	0.865	0.522	0.197	0.266	3.081	0.500
2001–02	0.744	0.912	0.149	0.188	0.803	0.566	0.129	0.223	3.176	0.566
2002–03	0.782	0.922	0.128	0.192	0.823	0.502	0.165	0.165	3.103	0.587
2003–04	0.761	0.917	0.155	0.233	0.856	0.467	0.176	0.219	2.893	0.589
2004–05	0.749	0.889	0.132	0.238	0.892	0.489	0.182	0.266	2.983	0.594
2005–06	0.738	0.901	0.119	0.241	0.882	0.506	0.145	0.265	3.154	0.612

Notes: 1. The factor loading of the eight port performance indicators for three different years is derived by the formula eigen vector = (factor loading)/ √(eigen value). Eigen value is the first value of the 'variance explained' column in the unrotated factor loading (pattern). 2. Explained variance as percentage of total.

Table 2.1(b). Rank of Weights of Port Performance Indicators: PCA

Year	TRT	PBWT	PITTWB	OSBD	BOR	BTR	PTOS	RRT
1985–86	7	6	8	2	5	4	3	1
1986–87	7	4	8	1	5	2	6	3
1987–88	8	5	7	1	6	2	4	3
1988–89	5	1	7	6	2	4	8	3
1989–90	7	8	4	2	5	1	6	3
1990–91	7	6	4	2	5	1	8	3
1991–92	6	4	7	2	3	1	8	5
1992–93	6	2	7	3	1	4	8	5
1993–94	6	1	8	4	2	5	7	3
1994–95	4	3	8	7	2	6	5	1
1995–96	1	2	8	6	3	5	7	4
1996–97	3	1	8	6	2	4	7	5
1997–98	5	1	7	4	2	3	8	6
1998–99	3	1	7	6	2	4	8	5
1999–00	3	2	7	6	1	4	8	5
2000–01	3	1	8	6	2	4	7	5
2001–02	3	1	7	6	2	4	8	5
2002–03	3	1	8	5	2	4	6	6
2003–04	3	1	8	5	2	4	7	6
2004–05	3	2	8	6	1	4	7	5
2005–06	3	1	8	6	2	4	7	5

ing PPI in the post-liberalisation era. But these two financial performance variables played key role in determining PPI in the pre-liberalisation period.

Fifth, Table 2.1(c) presents the values of the performance index of 12 major ports over three different time points. The coefficient of variation (CV) of PPI has substantially declined in 2005–06 (0.19) even after rising from 0.52 in 1985–86 to 0.68 in 1990–91. Thus, there has been a tendency toward equalisation of inter-port performance index after liberalisation. In some sense, this may be interpreted as reflecting a rise in competitiveness among Indian ports in the post-reform period.

Sixth, it is noted that those ports which are performing better are attached with economically prosperous hinterland and vice versa. It is argued that since overall performance of states like Gujarat, Tamil Nadu, Andhra Pradesh, Goa and Maharashtra are much better than that of West Bengal, Orissa, Karnataka and Kerala, performance of ports of the first group of states is ahead of those in the second group. In order of ranking, these ports are Chennai (in Tamil Nadu), Kandla (in Gujarat), Vizag (in Andhra Pradesh), Mormugao (in Goa) and Mumbai (in Maharashtra). Their current (2007–08) shares are as follows: Kandla 12.50 percent, Vizag 12.44 percent, Chennai 11.01 percent and Mumbai 10.99 percent. Table 2.1 (e) and Figure 2.1 present this picture more clearly. Therefore, it may not be out of merit to find some sort of a scale economy to exert its positive impact on the performance index.

Finally, ranks of individual ports in terms of individual performance indicators, given in Table 2.1(d), make it clear that except Chennai and Vizag, the other ports of the east coast have been gradually retreating in terms of most of the indicators. Kandla port except for the year 1989–90, always hovered around the top position. Port performance retrogression is very significant for New Mangalore, Jawaharlal Nehru and Haldia.

To conclude, according to the PPI in 2005–06, the three best performing ports are Chennai, Kandla and Vizag, and the worst three ports are Cochin, Paradip, and Jawaharlal Nehru. To be more specific, values of these scores are much more important than mere ranking. High variance in both PPI and individual factors, among other things, represent

Table 2.1(c). Port Performance Index (PPI): PCA

Year	Kandla	Mumbai	JN	Mormugao	NM	Cochin	Tuticorin	Chennai	Vizag	Paradip	Kolkata	Haldia	Mean	SD[1]	CV[2]
1985–86	13.30	8.05	*	11.06	4.65	2.66	6.27	9.16	7.85	3.37	0.88	9.25	6.95	3.61	0.52
1986–87	5.87	1.58	*	5.60	0.83	–1.14	0.42	2.39	3.48	1.36	–1.63	3.04	1.98	2.31	1.17
1987–88	1.66	–3.80	*	4.01	–1.30	–1.45	–1.67	0.13	0.16	0.77	–6.84	–0.35	–0.79	2.71	–3.43
1988–89	14.79	13.93	*	12.51	15.88	7.30	9.17	12.65	9.14	9.60	6.95	10.38	11.12	2.87	0.26
1989–90	4.22	3.50	–0.10	8.82	8.62	6.47	4.98	5.83	5.05	4.60	2.81	6.25	5.09	2.34	0.46
1990–91	5.08	2.08	0.38	8.24	7.10	3.40	3.75	4.54	4.06	2.62	–1.22	3.97	3.67	2.48	0.68
1991–92	9.96	2.35	2.80	9.71	7.48	2.36	4.53	5.27	6.70	4.58	–0.30	4.09	4.96	2.94	0.59
1992–93	14.46	7.47	6.22	14.51	8.58	5.41	8.81	9.17	10.75	8.40	3.13	8.73	8.80	3.17	0.36
1993–94	12.74	6.96	2.95	10.66	6.50	2.37	6.90	7.88	8.89	7.13	1.50	6.43	6.74	3.14	0.47
1994–95	16.47	12.08	14.13	8.72	7.42	4.70	8.38	11.38	10.74	11.00	7.62	10.77	10.28	3.04	0.30
1995–96	14.84	7.39	9.93	7.84	2.84	2.19	5.58	6.03	8.76	8.52	2.63	6.31	6.91	3.41	0.49
1996–97	12.81	8.21	5.29	6.95	2.76	2.76	5.51	8.04	6.85	5.07	2.15	4.75	5.93	2.83	0.48
1997–98	14.05	8.40	4.11	12.40	6.07	5.57	7.15	10.22	9.90	7.52	4.53	7.13	8.09	2.93	0.36
1998–99	16.95	10.55	6.89	12.65	8.81	7.34	10.61	14.05	11.66	9.03	8.15	9.98	10.56	2.80	0.27
1999–00	16.12	10.89	6.88	12.71	8.97	7.56	10.88	14.78	12.22	9.66	8.18	10.02	10.74	2.70	0.25
2000–01	15.34	12.77	6.95	12.79	9.13	7.98	11.13	15.67	12.80	9.89	9.22	10.68	11.20	2.63	0.24
2001–02	15.87	11.87	7.43	12.97	9.21	8.26	12.44	15.88	13.98	9.96	9.67	10.98	11.54	2.68	0.23
2002–03	16.26	11.92	7.67	11.22	10.28	8.82	12.56	14.90	13.55	9.98	9.92	11.29	11.53	2.38	0.21
2003–04	15.34	12.22	8.54	12.12	10.24	9.44	11.87	14.97	12.87	10.12	10.08	11.56	11.61	2.00	0.17
2004–05	15.81	12.45	8.96	11.87	10.12	8.78	12.24	15.19	14.22	10.17	10.13	12.15	11.84	2.23	0.19
2005–06	15.54	12.16	8.26	12.76	10.97	8.89	12.35	15.67	14.24	9.92	11.17	12.09	12.00	2.26	0.19

Notes: 1. Standard Deviation. 2. Coefficient of Variations. 3.* Not in operation. 4. JN and NM represent Jawaharlal Nehru and New Mangalore ports respectively.

Table 2.1(d). Rank of Ports in PPI

Year	Kandla	Mumbai	JN	Mormugao	NM	Cochin	Tuticorin	Chennai	Vizag	Paradip	Kolkata	Haldia
1985–86	1	5		2	8	10	7	4	6	9	11	3
1986–87	1	6		2	8	10	9	5	3	7	11	4
1987–88	2	10		1	7	8	9	5	4	3	11	6
1988–89	2	3		5	1	10	8	4	9	7	11	6
1989–90	9	10	12	1	2	3	7	5	6	8	11	4
1990–91	3	10	11	1	2	8	7	4	5	9	12	6
1991–92	1	11	9	2	3	10	7	5	4	6	12	8
1992–93	2	9	10	1	7	11	5	4	3	8	12	6
1993–94	1	6	10	2	8	11	7	4	3	5	12	9
1994–95	1	3	2	8	11	12	9	4	7	5	10	6
1995–96	1	6	2	5	10	12	9	8	3	4	11	7
1996–97	1	2	7	4	10	10	6	3	5	8	12	9
1997–98	1	5	12	2	9	10	7	3	4	6	11	8
1998–99	1	6	12	3	9	11	5	2	4	8	10	7
1999–00	1	5	12	3	9	11	6	2	4	8	10	7
2000–01	2	5	12	4	10	11	6	1	3	8	9	7
2001–02	2	6	12	4	10	11	5	1	3	8	9	7
2002–03	1	5	12	7	8	11	4	2	3	9	10	6
2003–04	1	4	12	5	8	11	6	2	3	9	10	7
2004–05	1	4	11	7	10	12	5	2	3	8	9	6
2005–06	2	6	12	4	9	11	5	1	3	10	8	7

Note: * Not in operation. 1. JN and NM represent Jawaharlal Nehru and New Mangalore ports respectively.

Table 2.1(e). Share of Major Ports in Total Port Traffic

Year	Kandla	Mumbai	JN	Mormugao	NM	Cochin	Tuticorin	Chennai	Ennore	Vizag	Paradip	Haldia	Kolkata
						(%)							
1985–86	13.78	20.32	*	13.47	3.08	4.41	3.53	15.17	*	13.3	2.78	6.66	3.48
1986–87	13.02	20.17	*	12	4.37	5.53	3.32	15.9	*	12.09	3.9	6.45	3.26
1987–88	13.43	21.97	*	9.9	4.54	5.05	3.16	16.95	*	11.42	3.86	6.45	3.26
1988–89	12.11	19.95	*	10.47	4.82	5.32	3.49	16.22	*	13.85	4.1	6.72	2.95
1989–90	12.82	18.8	0.47	9.6	5.19	4.82	3.61	16.22	*	14.31	4.19	7.01	2.94
1990–91	12.96	19.02	1.33	9.81	5.28	4.79	3.34	16.14	*	12.78	4.53	7.31	2.72
1991–92	13.41	16.76	1.78	9.64	5.28	4.78	3.75	15.99	*	13.74	4.66	7.56	2.66
1992–93	13.76	17.39	1.81	9.8	4.26	4.79	3.74	15.21	*	13.67	4.56	7.92	3.1
1993–94	13.69	17.05	1.89	10.46	4.82	4.26	3.74	14.83	*	14.3	4.65	7.43	2.89
1994–95	13.53	15.66	2.56	9.64	4.09	4.41	4.1	15.04	*	15.33	5.17	7.52	2.96
1995–96	14.1	15.76	3.19	8.41	4.13	5.34	4.32	14.28	*	15.25	5.23	7.15	2.84
1996–97	14.84	14.84	3.55	7.62	5.48	5.17	4.04	14.01	*	15.18	5.1	7.52	2.65
1997–98	15.46	12.76	3.54	8.42	6.07	4.9	3.97	14.12	*	14.31	5.29	8.03	3.16
1998–99	16.14	12.3	4.66	7.16	5.65	5.03	4.03	13.98	*	14.16	5.21	8.03	3.64
1999–00	17.05	11.18	5.51	6.75	6.47	4.71	3.68	13.77	*	14.25	5.22	7.62	3.79
2000–01	14.66	11.12	5.69	7.87	6.35	4.34	4.12	13.28	*	14.36	6.37	8.76	3.12
2001–02	13.12	9.19	7.83	7.97	6.09	4.19	4.53	12.56	1.18	15.42	7.35	8.70	1.87
2002–03	12.96	8.55	8.56	7.54	6.83	4.15	4.24	10.74	2.71	14.67	7.62	9.12	2.30
2003–04	12.04	8.70	9.05	8.08	7.74	3.94	3.97	10.65	2.69	13.84	7.34	9.45	2.52
2004–05	10.83	9.17	8.55	7.99	8.83	3.67	4.12	11.42	2.47	13.07	14.54	9.45	2.59
2005–06	10.84	10.44	8.91	7.48	8.14	3.29	4.05	11.16	2.17	13.18	7.82	9.97	2.55
2006–07	11.42	11.29	9.66	7.38	6.91	3.29	3.88	11.52	2.31	12.16	8.30	9.15	2.72
2007–08	12.50	10.99	10.74	6.77	6.94	3.05	4.14	11.01	2.23	12.44	8.17	8.39	2.65

Note: * Not in operation. 1. JN and NM represent Jawarlal Nehru and New Mangalore ports respectively.
Source: Ministry of Shipping, Road Transport and Highways, Government of India

Figure 2.1 Scatter of Port Traffic against PPI: 1985–86 and 2005–06

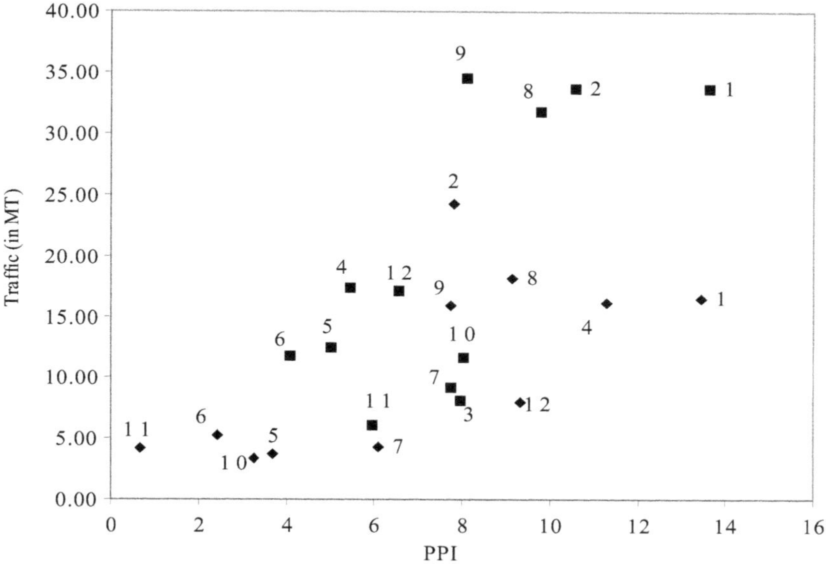

Legend: ◆ = 1985–86 ■ = 2005–06
Note: Serial numbers correspond to Table 2.1(c)

the level of differential inter-port performance. Except the first three ports, lower scores for the remaining ports represent their potential for further rise. To understand the nature of data, it may be useful to review the inter-port variations of each of the eight performance variables as they are given in the form of raw data over time. The values of mean, SD (standard deviation) and CV (coefficients of variation) of the raw indicators of port performance are given in Appendix 2.2. Except OSBD, BTR, PTOS, and RRT, CV for the rest of the variables have been rising over the years. Among these four variables, only RRT has become more equitable across the ports over time. That is, the value of CV of this variable has fallen from 0.64 in 1985–86 to 0.41 in 1991–92 to 0.38 in 2005–06. In contrast to this, PBWT displays the highest disparity – more than doubling from 0.33 in 1985–86 to 0.72 in 2005–06. This being a reasonably good indicator of port congestion suggests that there has been high variance in congestion across the ports.

Therefore, from the forgoing analysis, it may not be out of merit to find a causal relationship between performance and traffic, which we have dealt in the next section. This may be helpful in formulating the sequential priority of port policy and its overall direction.

2.3 Linkage between Traffic and Performance

As deemed by the present study, we have tried to find out the nature of the relationship between port performance, labour employment and capital with port traffic over different time spans. The estimated results of the OLS estimation of equation 2.3 are presented in Table 2.3 with the values of the coefficients, t-statistics, adjusted R^2, Durbin-Watson statistic (serial correlation), standard error of estimates and F values for two combinations of data sets - (i) 1985–86 and 2005–06 (case-1), and (ii) 1991–92 and 2005–06 (case-2) - separately. While the former explains the causality between endogenous and exogenous variables over an interval of 21 years, the later case evaluates the immediate impact of trade liberalisation undertaken in July 1991. In case 1, Kolkata port was omitted as an outlier and Jawaharlal Nehru was excluded because the port was not in operation in 1985–86. In case 2, both Kolkata and Mumbai ports came out as outliers on the basis of Cook's distance statistic (Cook and Weisberg, 1982). Hence, values of the parameters are estimated after omitting these two ports. Regression results are highly satisfactory. A look at the correlation matrices given in Table 2.2 makes certain features about the independent variable obvious. First, in no situation, L and PPI are significantly correlated. Second, in one situation (case 1, 1985–86), K is significantly correlated with L. Interestingly the same correlation in 1991–92 is also marginally significant. Finally, K does not cause any significantly high correlation with PPI in any year. This creates a ground for including K as an independent variable with PPI and L in both pair of years. Therefore, no correlation coefficient is significant enough to warrant the presence multicolinearity among the variables.

For each pair of years, we have tested four combinations of independent variables. Some findings are as follows. First, it is observed from Table 2.3 that in both cases best results, in relative term are obtained from the combination of PPI and L and time dummy as can be

Table 2.2 Correlation Matrix

(a) Case 1 (1985–86 and 2005–06)

	PPI (05–06)	L (05–06)	K (00–01)	PPI (85–86)	L (85–86)	K (85–86)
PPI (05–06)	1	0.311	0.517	0.538	0.375	0.703
		p=.351	p=.104	p=.088	p=.256	p=.016
L (05–06)		1	0.443	0.113	0.646	0.273
			p=.173	p=.742	p=.032	p=.416
K (05–06)			1	0.391	0.164	0.307
				p=.234	p=.630	p=.359
PPI (85–86)				1	−0.213	0.065
					p=.530	p=.850
L (85–86)					1	0.698
						p=.017
K (85–86)						1

(b) Case 2 (1991–92 and 2005–06)

	PPI (05–06)	L (05–06)	K (05–06)	PPI (91–92)	L (91–92)	K (91–92)
PPI (05–06)	1	0.322	0.528	0.380	0.276	0.525
		p=.308	p=.078	p=.223	p=.385	p=.079
L (05–06)		1	0.452	−0.373	0.946	0.413
			p=.140	p=.233	p=.000	p=.183
K (05–06)			1	−0.157	0.596	0.993
				p=.627	p=.041	p=.000
PPI (91–92)				1	−0.388	−0.125
					p=.212	p=.698
L (91–92)					1	0.571
						p=.052
K (91–92)						1

Notes: 1. L = Labour, K= Capital, PPI = Port Performance Index. 2. N = 22 in case 1 and =24 in case 2. 3. Correlation coefficients are significant at $p<0.05$

Table 2.3 Regression Results

(a) Case 1 (1985–86 and 2005–06)

Dependent variable	Independent variable	Coefficient	t-values	Adj. R^2	SEE	F	DW	SC	N
Traffic (Y)	Constant	8.057	1.476	0.760	0.331	16.036	2.240	–0.176	20
	Ln(PPI)	0.530	2.458						
	Ln(L)	0.308	2.463						
	Ln(K)	0.205	0.697						
	D	0.626	3.830						
Traffic (Y)	Constant	0.139	0.028	0.684	0.380	14.726	1.968	–0.026	20
	Ln(L)	0.241	1.722						
	Ln(K)	0.645	2.409						
	D	0.577	3.099						
Traffic (Y)	Constant	11.821	15.108	0.768	0.326	21.924	2.327	–0.229	20
	Ln(PPI)	0.621	3.692						
	Ln(L)	0.365	3.893						
	D	0.671	4.543						
Traffic (Y)	Constant	0.790	0.150	0.684	0.380	14.703	2.189	–0.133	20
	Ln(PPI)	0.414	1.715						
	Ln(K)	0.675	2.627						
	D	0.500	2.807						

(b) Case 2 (1991–92 and 2005–06)

Dependent variable	Independent variable	Coefficient	t-values	Adj. R^2	SEE	F	DW	SC	N
Traffic (Y)	Constant	13.196	3.398	0.789	0.307	18.716	2.312	–0.258	20
	Ln(PPI)	0.692	3.581						
	Ln(L)	0.643	5.638						
	Ln(K)	–0.154	–0.807						
	D	0.228	1.404						
Traffic (Y)	Constant	7.251	1.567	0.632	0.404	11.893	2.503	–0.352	20
	Ln(L)	0.695	4.657						
	Ln(K)	0.148	0.655						
	D	0.523	2.837						
Traffic (Y)	Constant	10.145	11.577	0.793	0.303	25.289	2.314	–0.249	20
	Ln(PPI)	0.623	3.634						
	Ln(L)	0.621	5.674						
	D	0.238	1.488						
Traffic (Y)	Constant	12.567	1.893	0.382	0.524	4.911	2.480	–0.267	20
	Ln(PPI)	0.830	2.532						
	Ln(K)	0.111	0.350						
	D	0.101	0.367						

Notes: 1. Kolkata port was deleted as outlier following Cook's Distance Statistic and Jawaharlal Nehru Port was excluded as the port was not in operation in 1985–86. 2. In Case 2, Mumbai and Kolkata ports were deleted as outliers following Cook's Distance Statistic. 3. SEE, F, DW, SC and N stand for standard error of estimate, F value, Durbin Watson statistic, serial correlation, and number of observations. 4. D = Time Dummy (=1 for later year, = 0 for other). 5. Each port's capital was deflated by gross domestic capital formation deflator (base: 1980–81=100), and accumulated over time up to the concerned time point.

judged by the standard error of estimate (SEE). Interestingly, the inclusion of K as a third variable not only marginally reduces the value of adjusted R^2, increases the SEE but it also reduces the value of F-statistic. And while doing so it fails to come out with any significance as can be judged from lower t-values. Second, the traditional combination of L and K makes the regression results substantially poor. Third, as analysed by us earlier, the best result is obtained only with the combination of PPI and L with the presence of time dummy in both cases

Given the limited number of cross-section observations, the high values of adjusted R^2 (0.768 and 0.793) along with the required values of DW and F-Statistic confirm the fact that only two factors, performance index and labour employment, explain a very high proportion of traffic across Indian ports.

Port traffic is highly contingent upon port performance, the coefficient (or elasticity) of which is not only very high (0.621 in case 1 and 0.623 in case 2) and positive but also significant at 1 percent level ($t = 3.692$ in case 1 and 3.634 in case 2). The elasticities of traffic with respect to PPI for both cases indicate that every 1 percent increase of PPI causes 0.62 percent higher traffic. Despite the marginal difference between the coefficients of PPI in the two cases, there is still scope for further development of performance levels of ports in the coming years.

We have also found positive and significant association of labour employment over time with traffic. The coefficient of labour in case 1 (0.365) is lower than that of case 2 (0.621). While in case 1, for 1 percent increase in labour employment, traffic increases by 0.37 percent, but for the same increase of labour input in case 2, traffic is higher by 0.62 percent. It is also found that the elasticity of output with respect to PPI has been higher than that of L in both cases. This has become more transparent in case 2 where labour endowment appears to be significant due to the fact that in the post-liberalisation period, total labour force of major ports has been declining fast. This may also be substantiated with the help of Table 2.4. It is seen that annual growth rate of cargo of almost all major ports has been much higher than that of labour. In fact, except Jawaharlal Nehru, New Mangalore, Tuticorin, and Haldia, all the major ports have registered negative growth of labour force. The above relationship also indicates that a few ports need to consolidate their labour pool.

Inclusion of the time dummy has benefited us in understanding the production system in port between each pair of years. As can be found from Table 2.3, the value of the coefficient of the dummy variable is high, positive and significant between 1985–86 and 2005–06. But, as expected, it was insignificant between the later pair of years. This suggests that no significant breakthrough has occurred in India's port performance behaviour ever since the reform in 1991. Alternatively, the significant positive value of the time dummy for the earlier pair of years implies that natural rate of progression has occurred over a time lag of 21 years.

It may be concluded that to attain higher traffic, ports obviously should give highest priority to their performance by improving operational performance factors like PBWT, TRT, and asset performance

Table 2.4. Average Annual Growth Rates of Cargo and Employment

Ports	1985–86 – 2005–06		1991–92 – 2005–06	
	Cargo	Employment	Cargo	Employment
		(%)		
Kandla	8.93	–1.10	8.47	–2.11
Mumbai	4.09	–1.83	4.88	–2.16
Jawaharlal Nehru	296.91	3.13	89.59	3.56
Mormugao	4.84	–0.93	7.85	–0.89
New Mangalore	41.77	2.49	22.62	3.10
Cochin	8.22	–1.80	6.16	–2.17
Tuticorin	15.30	0.71	13.71	0.96
Chennai	8.02	–1.39	6.34	–1.75
Vizag	12.54	–2.65	11.38	–3.85
Paradip	44.80	–2.13	25.27	–2.45
Kolkata	21.51	–3.72	18.33	–4.76
Haldia	7.98	0.65	11.39	0.27

Note: * Initial year is 1989–90

Source: Ministry of Shipping, Road Transport and Highways, Government of India

indicators like BOR. These three most important determinants of port performance as appeared in the post-liberalisation period from principal component analysis are related to the degree of port congestion. Hence, for attracting higher traffic, ports have to monitor these crucial factors very closely so that higher efficiency induces higher traffic. On the other hand, under the present trend of traffic, there is sufficient hint in favour of such policy measures by which to create further port capacity.

Therefore, the use of a quasi-production function demonstrates that port performance index and labour endowment alone explain a very large proportion of traffic in Indian ports.

2.4 Policy Implications

The findings of this study, among other things, have strong implications for future policy changes pertaining to Indian ports, and as a matter of fact, to the ports of developing countries in the era of globalisation. It is observed that Indian ports need to emphasise more on 'de-congestion' for making exports competitive. The lagging ports may not be able to improve their performance instantaneously because the resilient external factors, which have very strong influence on performance, are beyond the control of the port authorities. In general, a nationally favourable environment would be more congenial for improving port performance levels before undertaking any drastic policy measures. Sometimes lack of coordination between railways, roadways and coastal shipping authorities put the port in a very dismal condition, which in subsequent periods negatively impacts upon the growth of export by raising transaction costs.

It has been observed that there has been a shift in long distance coastal cargo transportation from ports to railways and/or roads due to the poor performance and differential freight systems across ports. The average ship turnaround time in 2005–06 was 3.63 days. It was even higher, 8.1 days, in 1990–91 (Government of India, 1998). Compared to Singapore's port where the turnaround time is counted in hours, Indian ports are just globally uncompetitive in terms of any crude measure. According to Peters (1997): '... the reason for this sorry state of affairs is that our ports were designed to handle specific categories of cargo which have declined over time while other types of traffic have gained importance. But the port's berth configurations were not adjusted to the new categories of cargo. In almost all ports productivity levels are extremely low by international standards. Due to this, the added costs to our exporters and importers are substantial'.

There is no denying the fact that the question of efficiency is inextricably linked to the appropriateness of the chosen technology, and more often than not the fault may lie in the institutional preparedness for scientific management which is necessary for the smooth functioning of the new technology. As for the manufacturing sector so also for the port sector, economists in the developed countries have long been persuaded about the role of R&D in fostering appropriate technological manoeuvre which in turn helps achieve faster all-round productivity growth in an economy (Giriliches, 1986; Nadiri, 1980; Ishikawa, 1981; Ghosh and Neogi, 1993). But the governments as well as the economists of the developing countries bothered little about the role technology can play in integrating manufacturing, awareness for trade, transaction and trade itself. India is no exception. Port sector in India is not only one of the most ignored sectors but also technological obsolescence epitomises the official attention received by Indian ports since the First Five Year Plan in 1951 to the beginning of the Eleventh Plan in 2007. It is in very recent years that failure in the export front has been sporadically linked to the non-price factors in general and inefficiency of ports in particular. Effective utilisation of existing facilities in ports not only helps tackle congestion more efficiently but it has also a tremendous spill over effect among manufacturers enabling them to turn to overseas markets. Despite tremendous data limitation relating to technological level of Indian ports, we have been able to present in Table 2.5 some information about the equipment and its utilisation rates across the major ports. The argument is not just that the utilisation rates of all the three types of cranes for handling general cargo are unequivocally sub-optimal. It rather implicitly suggests the level of obsolescence of equipment in use in Indian ports. Even the Tenth Five Year Plan (1997–2002) acknowledges this:

> ... equipment utilisation has been low in most of the major ports. Low productivity is mainly due to the operational constraints such as equipment breakdown, time spent on service and power failures, etc. Over-aging of installed equipments is another area of concern. Out of the total fleet strength, 88 percent of wharf cranes, 66 percent of mobile cranes, and 31 percent of fork lift trucks have crossed their economic life.

The net result of all this is that some ports handle much less cargo than what they did six decades ago. Interestingly, the same conclusion was reached by Haralambides and Behrens (2000). According to them, Indian ports are currently characterized by the existence of obsolete and poorly maintained equipment, hierarchical and bureaucratic management structures, excessive labour, and in general, an institutional framework that is considerably in variance with Government's overall economic objectives.

Realising urgent need for inter- and intra- port competition to attain higher performance level, the Government has invited the private sector to finance new port facilities (Government of India, 1999; 2006a). To attract private sector investments, India has adopted Public – Private Partnership (PPP) in port sector (Government of India, 2006a). Success to date is not unsatisfactory. According to Government of India (2006b):

> Since the announcement of the guidelines for private sector participation in order to promote modernisation and development in the port sector, 13 projects with private sector participation has become operational, and 4 projects are under implementation. These 17 projects involve an investment of Rs. 61.30 billion. About 20 projects involving more than Rs. 44.42 billion of private investment are under consideration.

Traditionally, the ownership of ports has been dominated by the public sector. But privatisation of port facilities and services has now gathered momentum in India. An enabling policy framework (see Box 2.1) has already been put in place. Depending on the nature of facility/service, private operators can enter into a service contract, a management con-

Table 2.5. Average Utilisation of General Cargo Handling Equipment

(%)

Major Ports[1]	Wharf Cranes[2]			Mobile Cranes			Fork Lifts		
	1985–86	1991–92	2005–06	1985–86	1991–92	2005–06	1985–86	1991–92	2005–06
Kandla	29.17	30.14	56.26	5.28	2.92		24.31	27.22	44.39
Mumbai	18.19	17.50	18.98	24.44	17.22	16.23	35.97	24.72	22.18
Mormugao	15.69	24.17		4.03	9.58	4.42	10.69	4.58	12.28
New Mangalore	3.33	4.31	7.12	4.03	2.78		6.39	3.19	10.89
Cochin	9.44	6.94	6.34	21.94	15.97	12.37	16.94	18.61	23.25
Tuticorin	7.92	22.08	32.92	3.47	14.58	3.19	5.00	10.97	
Chennai	57.36	38.47	12.31	47.08	35.28	34.30	46.67	37.50	16.07
Vizag	17.22	25.97	35.11	23.61	11.81	35.18	21.39	18.61	19.42
Paradip[3]	13.89	38.33	26.30	13.89	17.64	3.34	4.86	19.03	6.34
Kolkata[4]	29.72	22.36	17.24	34.44	30.42	42.78	36.25	35.97	36.92

Notes: 1. Jawaharlal Nehru and Haldia ports were omitted due to lack of required data. 2. Counts only electric wharf cranes of 3–10 tonnes. 3. There were no 3–10 tonnes wharf cranes working, and all were above 10 tonnes cranes. 4. Only 2–10 tonnes wharf cranes were considered.

Source: Ministry of Shipping, Road Transport and Highways, Government of India

Box 2.1: National Maritime Development Progromme (NMDP)

For the first time a comprehensive National Maritime Development Policy is formulated in order to facilitate private investment, improve service quality and promote competitiveness. The policy also aims at encouraging more investments in port projects at substantially higher levels to meet the medium and long term objectives. With this objective, the Department of Shipping in the Ministry of Shipping, Road Transport and Highways, Government of India, is responsible to implement the National Maritime Development Programme (NMDP) to complement the National Maritime Policy (NMP) by identifying specific schemes/projects and other measures which are necessary to give a concrete shape to the vision and strategy laid down in the policy document upto 2011–12.

The Government of India has undertaken the NMDP with an investment of Rs. 610 billion to boost infrastructure at major ports in the next ten years. Under the NMDP, 228 projects have been identified for implementation in two phases through public-private partnership (PPP). By identifying specific projects and other measures, the NMDP will over the next 10 years give a concrete shape to the vision and strategy of the NMP. The envisaged investment for these projects is estimated at Rs 610 billion, of this, Rs 392.38 billion will come from the private sector, Rs 114.45 billion through budgetary support and Rs 50.78 billion from port trusts' internal resources.

The programme is being implemented through PPP. Public investments is sought primarily for common user infrastructure facilities in the ports like deepening and maintenance of port channels, construction of breakwaters, internal circulation systems of cargo within the ports, rail and road connectivity from ports to hinterland, etc. Private investments are allowed in the areas where operations are primarily commercial in nature like construction, management and operation of berths, terminals, among others.

Source: Government of India (2006b)

tract, a concession agreement or a divestiture to operate port services. Areas that have been opened up to the private sector on Build-Operate-Transfer (BOT) basis include construction of cargo handling berths and dry-docks, container terminals and warehousing facilities and ship repair facilities. However, port sector needs more investments to sustain India's growth. To fill-up the gap, about US$ 18 billion has been earmarked for the port sector in the 11th Five Year Plan (2007–2012) (Government of India, 2007).

2.5 Concluding Remarks

This chapter uses some individual port performance indicators, which are largely internal to each of the ports, for explaining port throughput. These factors alone explain a substantial proportion of traffic. Hence, even though we did not consider the external factors, it may be concluded that performance does lead to increased traffic. Efficient management can lead to significant increases in port throughput, which may then increase the demand for port services. If a port performs better by improving its operational and asset performance initially then it is going to get higher traffic. However, we have not considered here the spatial concentration of manufacturing activities in and around the ports, differential geographical attributes, logistics networks, and differential nation-wide infrastructure stocks associated with each region which may have very substantial bearings on port traffic. The findings of this chapter may be further substantiated incorporating these exogenous factors and also be used to find out empirical causality between port performance and port traffic, which will help us evaluate the performance of the port sector in general framework under liberal economic regime. This has been dealt in the next chapter.

Appendix 2.1 Definition of Performance Indicators

1. Ship Turn-Round Time is the duration of the vessel's stay in port and is calculated from the time of arrival to the time of departure.
2. Pre-Berthing Waiting Time is the time a ship has to wait before getting entry into a berth.
3. Percentage of Idle Time at Berth to Time at Working Berth is the ratio of total idle time to total working time while a ship is in the port.
4. Output per Ship Berth Day means total tonnage handled, or distributed over the total number of ship berth days.
5. Berth Throughput Rate means total cargo handled by a berth in a port.
6. Berth Occupancy Rate is the time that a berth is occupied by ships.
7. Operating Surplus per tonne of Cargo Handled derives from total operating surplus divided by total tonnage of cargo handled by the port.
8. Rate of Return on Turnover derives from operating surplus divided by operating income of a port.

Appendix 2.2 Port Performance Indicators: Mean, SD[1] and CV[2]

Performance variables	1985–86 Mean	1991–92 Mean	2005–06 Mean	1985–86 SD	1991–92 SD	2005–06 SD	1985–86 CV	1991–92 CV	2005–06 CV
TRT (days)	10.27	6.37	3.63	2.75	1.82	1.65	0.27	0.29	0.32
PBWT (days)	2.92	1.46	1.11	0.97	0.74	1.24	0.33	0.51	0.72
PITTWB (%)	35.73	34.17	30.27	11.74	11.66	11.39	0.33	0.34	0.38
OSBD (tonnes)	3073.45	4458.42	5790.71	1773.89	2506.94	2601.82	0.58	0.56	0.45
BOR (%)	70.40	66.87	73.20	8.34	12.73	15.15	0.12	0.19	0.21
BTR (%)	126.48	155.91	172.10	108.05	124.90	111.32	0.85	0.80	0.65
PTOS (Rs.)	1.21	2.34	5.16	0.97	1.27	4.89	0.81	0.54	0.95
RRT (%)	27.07	27.47	37.04	17.33	11.33	17.77	0.64	0.41	0.38

Notes: 1. Standard Deviation, 2. Coefficient of Variation

Causality between Port Performance and Port Traffic

3.1 Introduction

Our main purpose in this chapter is to analyse the causality between performance and traffic of Indian ports over the period from 1985 to 2005. There are some studies, which have tried to understand the relation between a country's openness, port performance and port traffic, but none has touched upon the empirical causality between port performance and port traffic. Several reasons explain the choice of the Indian port sector. First, the port sector in several erstwhile developing countries has been undergoing transformation from a subsistence infrastructure resource into a more capital intensive, commercially oriented facility during the last two decades. On the other hand, the Government of India has lately thought about taking some steps leading to deregulation of country's port sector. Indian ports are currently characterised by the existence of obsolete and poorly maintained equipment, hierarchical and bureaucratic management structures, weak coordination between the port trusts and users of the ports, lack of synchronisation of working times, excessive labour, and in general, an institutional framework that is considerably in variance with government's overall economic objectives (De Monie, 1995; Peters, 1997; Haralambides and Behrens, 2000; IDFC, 2001; De, 2003). Second, considering the country's entry into the second stage of reform, the analysis will help assess potential benefits of moving to a deregularised port sector under a liberal trading regime when more than 80 percent of the country's international trade pass through seaports. For instance, if performance stimulates traffic, then the benefits of performance augmenting factors might be responsible not only for redistribution of existing traffic but also for attracting new manufacturers and suppliers. There are ample examples to show that even if a country produces technologically advanced quality goods (pure theory of trade), non-price factors like transport costs and facilities often work as decisive deterrence to trade. So, causal inspection of trends of country's overseas trade suggests the need for an investigation into the linkages between port performance and port traffic.

Rigorous theoretical arguments could be advanced in support of a possible 'causality' between performance and traffic. The nature of this causality is essentially an empirical question. There are three basic reasons why the study of causality for understanding the economic functioning of ports will be highly instructive for future policy in an era of worldwide laissez faire.

The first relates to the very nature of the subject as an inseparable part of social decision making. Here we deal with extremely imperfect knowledge and information which give birth to conclusions that we can not establish with precision. In sharp contrast, in physical science, there are many 'laws' which we can call with precision as 'universal'. Hence the application even of a partly gross technique of identifying some relationship between the concerned variables as 'prior' or 'after' would certainly make one millionth of a step forward in understanding the relevant thrust of policy (Hicks, 1979).

Second, in understanding the nature of the relationship among the relevant variables, one must have to bring in 'time' into the framework. Unlike other fields of knowledge, the economists are mainly concerned with the 'present' time, while the historians with the whole of recorded history – the 'past'. Interestingly, the very 'present' is really fleeting: one does not have time to think about it until it becomes 'past'– a past that is measurable either in terms of second, minutes, hours, years or centuries. This means that even economic logic is (should, because one major purpose of such study is to enlighten the future policy makers) highly linked with the past and also with the future. But it is with the past that he/she has to begin. This series of past information through the present that help make generalisations for predicting the future, guide the policy makers in undertaking relevant planning. In the true sense of the term, 'time' in such a framework is one of long run. But in reality, we do have to sometimes contend with information in the past which can not go beyond a couple of decades. That may impose some amount of limitation in the efficacy of the estimated parameters; nonetheless it would certainly be an additional advantage over working in a cross-section framework.

Third, unlike other subjects of social science, economics is specially concerned with the making of decisions (and hence guiding future course of actions through relevant policies) and also with the consequences that follow from these decisions. There are profound implications involved in this process of policy making and subsequent economic development. This is more desirable than a 'counter-factual' logic of defending an ad hoc policy.[1]

Investigating this causality may be highly paying in terms of future policy. For example, if, under certain conditions, there is enough evidence towards the fact that performance precedes traffic, then performance-augmenting factors should get priority in the chain of policy making such that higher traffic will be a resultant of better policy induced investment. At a later stage, this will improve trading status of the nation. If, on the other hand, it is seen that traffic appears to cause performance, then reducing trade restrictions and transaction costs may encourage adoption of performance augmenting technology, which in its turn will have positive impact upon traffic and hence on international trade.

Four mutually exclusive causal relationships can be contemplated. These are: unidirectional causality from performance to traffic or traffic to performance, no causality in either direction and causality in both directions. Each of these cases has different implications for port policy.

1 Let us take an example: the study of the past, with the object of finding out not only what has happened, but also helps us understand why it has happened. If the study is successful, we may be able to state a 'cause': A caused B, i.e., in historical series, A is prior to B; but this is not absolute. There are four distinguishable elements in the assertion of (separable) causation of B by A: (1) A existed (2) B existed (3) the hypothetical situation in which A did not exist, ceteris paribus, can be constructed (4) if that situation existed, at time T, B would not have occurred.

The organisation of the chapter is as follows. Section 3.2 deals with the data and methodology. Section 3.3 talks about performance of major ports of India. Section 3.4 tests the causality between port performance and port traffic. Finally, policy implications and concluding remarks are briefed in Section 3.5.

3.2 Data and Methodology

In general, port facility can be taken as infrastructure input from the supply side. We have used here performance index of Indian ports, which was developed in Chapter 2. As reported in Chapter 2, port performance index (PPI), which comprises indicators like operational performance (ship turnaround time (TRT), pre-berthing waiting time (PBWT), and percentage of idle time at berth to time at working berth (PITTWB)), asset performance (output per ship berth day (OSBD), berth throughput rate (BTR), and berth occupancy rate (BOR)) and financial performance (operating surplus per tonne of cargo handled (PTOS) and rate of return on turnover (RRT)) for 12 major ports over a period of 21 years starting from 1985 to 2005. The details of PPI and its formulations are explained in Chapter 2, which do not need any further discussion here.

To determine the causal relationship which best describes the empirical reality in Indian port sector, we attempt to apply some econometric tests. Unit root tests, Cointegration tests, and Granger causality tests are conducted in a sequential manner to judge the nature and strength of this causality in Section 3.3.

The choice of the initial year (1985–86) is influenced by the fact that since the mid-80s, India embarked for the first time upon a path of trade liberalisation with special emphasis on the telecommunication and electronics sectors. In 1991–92, India undertook economic reform as explicit state policy, which began with the announcement of the new Industrial Policy in July, 1991. A break at 1991–92 helps evaluate the nature of the relationship among the variables in the post-liberalisation period.

The main data for this study have been collected from various issues of (i) Basic Ports Statistics of India, and (ii) Transport Statistics of India - all published by the Ministry of Shipping, Road Transport and Highways, Government of India. This data set is supplemented by several issues of 'Major Ports of India: A Profile', published by the Indian Ports Association, New Delhi.

3.3 Measures of Port Performance

As the objective of this study is to examine the causality between port performance and port traffic, it considers only those indicators, which are directly linked with port performance. To understand the impact of such indicators, it is necessary to identify the factor(s), which lead to influence most on the overall performance of a particular port. Hence, we consider PPI of Indian major ports, which was developed in Chapter 2, comprising indicators of operational performance (TRT, PBWT, PITTWB), asset performance (OSBD, BTR, BOR) and financial performance (PTOS, RRT). Following the Chapter 2, we have taken eight performance variables of major ports over the period from 1985 to 2005. For the sake of better understanding of the environment, findings of PPI, which already reported in Chapter 2, are briefly reproduced here.

First, as we have seen earlier, we have not found a single variable that has emerged as the most influential factor in all the years. The variables, which have emerged as influential determining factors before 1991, came out as less important factors in the post-liberalisation period. However, looking at the overall consecutive good rankings of TRT, BTR and PBWT during the period, it is felt that these variables have played influential role in determining the performance of individual ports.

Second, PBWT, BOR, TRT and BTR have been found to be important determinant of performance in the post-liberalisation period during 1991-92 to 2005-2006. Thus, two each of the operational performance indicators (TRT and PBWT) and asset performance indicators (BTR, BOR) have emerged as decisive factors in determining the PPI in the post-liberalisation period.

Third, two of the operational performance indicators (PBWT and TRT), and one asset performance indicator (BOR) became the first three important factors in terms of weights in determining performance of an individual port in 2005–06.

Fourth, unlike popular belief, financial performance indicators like PTOS and RRI have emerged as factors of low importance in determining PPI in the post-liberalisation era. But, these two financial performance variables played key role in determining PPI in the pre-liberalisation period.

Fifth, the coefficient of variation (CV) of PPI, reported in Appendix 2.2, has substantially declined in 2005–06 (0.19) even after rising from 0.52 in 1985–86 to 0.68 in 1990–91. Thus, there has been a tendency toward equalisation of inter-port performance index after liberalisation. In some sense, this may be interpreted as reflecting a rise in competitiveness among Indian ports in the post-reform period.

Sixth, it is noted that those ports, which are performing better are attached with economically prosperous hinterland and vice versa. It is argued that since overall performance of states like Gujarat, Tamil Nadu, Andhra Pradesh, Goa and Maharashtra are much better than that of West Bengal, Orissa, Karnataka and Kerala (Dutt and Ravallion, 1998; Ghosh *et al.* 1998; Ghosh and De, 1998, 2000a, 2004, 2005a, 2005b), performance of ports of the first group of states is ahead of those in the second group. In order of ranking, these ports are Chennai (in Tamil Nadu), Kandla (in Gujarat), Vizag (in Andhra Pradesh), Mormugao (in Goa) and Mumbai (in Maharashtra). These five ports together contribute more than 65 percent of total Indian port traffic in recent periods.

To conclude, according to the PPI in 2005–06, the three best performing ports are Chennai, Kandla and Vizag, and the worst three ports are Cochin, New Mangalore, and Paradip. To be more specific, values of these scores are much more important than mere ranking. High variance in both PPI and individual factors, among other things, represent the level of differential inter-port performance. Except the first three ports, lower scores for the remaining ports represent their potential for further rise. To understand the nature of data, it may be useful to review the inter-port variations of each of the eight performance variables as they are given in the form of raw data over time. The values of mean, SD and CV of the raw indicators of port performance are given in Appendix 2.2 of Chapter 2. Except OSBD, BTR, PTOS, and RRT, CV for the rest of the variables have been rising over the years. Among these four variables, only RRT has become more equitable across the ports over time. That is, the value of CV of this variable has fallen from 0.64 in 1985–86 to 0.41 in 1991–92 to 0.38 in 2005–06. In contrast to this, PBWT displays the highest disparity – more than doubling from 0.33 in 1985–86 to 0.72 in 2005–06. This being a reasonably good indicator of port congestion suggests that there has been high variance in congestion across the ports.

Therefore, from the forgoing analysis, it may not be out of merit to find a causal relationship between performance and traffic. This may be helpful in formulating the sequential priority of port policy and its overall direction.

3.4 Causality between Performance and Traffic

To judge the nature and strength of the causal relationship between performance and traffic, Unit root tests, Cointegration tests, and Granger causality tests are conducted in a sequential manner.

The analysis proceeds sequentially in several steps. Since standard Granger causality tests presuppose that the data are stationary, investigating data stationarity properties constitutes the first phase of the analysis. If the data are non-stationary, they must be differenced enough to achieve stationarity. The specific form of the Granger causality test also depends on whether the data are cointegrated. For example, if the data series in a specific case are cointegrated, then an error correction model is an appropriate model of short run dynamics

(Engle and Granger, 1987). In this case the Granger causality test must include an error correction term as an explanatory variable. This error term restores relevant information that has been lost due to differencing the data and represents the error from a model using non-differenced data. However, if the data are non-stationary but not cointegrated, then Granger causality tests only require that the data be differenced sufficiently to achieve stationarity. Hence, to test the direction of causal relationship between performance and traffic of Indian ports, we shall first test the order of integration of the variables and then perform Granger causality test.

3.4.1 Unit Root Tests

In order to test the order of integration of the variables, three simple relations that may be used to represent many economic time series are the random walk, random walk with a drift and trend-stationary processes. All these three models are nested in the following equation.

$$\Delta Y_t = \mu + \beta t + (\rho - 1) Y_{t-1} + e_t \tag{3.1}$$

which is used for the Dickey-Fuller unit root test. Under the null hypothesis of a unit root, if ρ is close to unity, then the coefficient, $(\rho-1)$, will not be significantly different from zero. If there is no unit root, Y is said to be stationary in the levels, or integrated of order zero (denoted by I(0)). If there is a unit root, but differencing the series once makes it stationary, then it is said to be integrated of order one, denoted by I(1). The critical t values, for the tests, were calculated by Monte Carlo simulation in Fuller (1976), because the distribution is not standard. In addition to testing for the unit root, equation (3.1) will establish if there is a deterministic trend $(\beta \neq 0)$ and/or a drift $(\mu \neq 0)$. The error term, e_t, represents white noise. If Y_t is a first order autoregressive process (AR(1)), then the single lagged value of the dependent variable will be sufficient to ensure this condition. If the process is not AR(1), then m additional difference terms will need to be added to (3.1) to make e_t white noise. Thus the new equation becomes which is the equation of Augmented Dickey-Fuller (ADF) test.

$$\Delta Y_t = \mu + \beta t + (\rho - 1)\, Y_{t-1} + \sum_{i=1}^{m} \rho_j \Delta Y_{t-j} + e_t \qquad (3.2)$$

In the pertinent case, ADF test is used to test the null hypothesis (H_0: Y_t non-stationary) of a unit root for each of the major ports except Jawaharlal Nehru for 21 years period from 1985–86 to 2005–06 on the considered data series, namely, port performance index and port traffic.[2] This test involves a regression of the variable in a series (here traffic and PPI) against their lagged values, lagged difference terms and, as an option, a time trend. The test is carried out on traffic and PPI separately at level, and then at first difference and so on. The null hypothesis of a unit root is rejected if the parameter (ρ-1) is negative and significantly different from zero. Estimated test results are reported in Table 3.1. Although in this particular case we are considering parametric test, we have given Phillips-Perron test results in Appendix 3.1 for comparison.[3] Test results for all major ports in case of performance overwhelmingly reject null hypothesis of a unit root. This clearly shows that this data series are stationary at level (I(0)) with varied levels of significance. However, opposite results are obtained in case of port traffic. Here, test results fail to reject the null hypothesis of a unit root except Mumbai and Vizag at the level, and this indicates that traffic of major ports of India are non-stationary at level except Vizag and Mumbai. As a corollary, we have done a regression of the first difference of this particular data series and found that the null hypothesis of a unit root is rejected for all the ports at first difference and hence there is no requirement for further differencing of the data series.

To conclude, port performance data series are stationary at I(0), or integrated of order zero with varied levels of significance whereas port traffic series are non-stationary at I(0) but stationary at first differences, or integrated of order one, I(1).

2 We have not considered Jawaharlal Nehru in this causality test because the port became operational only since 1989 whereas all other ports are functioning before 1985–86.

3 Phillips and Perron (1988) propose a non-parametric method for controlling higher-order serial correlation in a series.

Table 3.1. Results of Augmented Dickey–Fuller (ADF) Test

(a) Port Performance

Ports	ADF[1]	MCV[2]	LD[3]	ADF[4]
Kandla	–3.845*	–3.382	1	–4.188**
Mumbai	–4.242**	–3.873	1	–
Mormugao	–4.240**	–3.873	1	–
New Mangalore	–5.593***	–5.115	2	–
Cochin	–4.137**	–3.927	2	–
Tuticorin	–3.734*	–3.411	2	–4.389**
Chennai	–4.566**	–3.927	2	–
Vizag	–3.949**	–3.873	1	–
Paradip	–4.481**	–3.873	1	–
Kolkata	–4.658**	–3.927	2	–
Haldia	–3.456*	–3.411	2	–3.912**

(b) Port Traffic

Ports	ADF[1]	MCV[2]	LD[3]	ADF[4]
Kandla	–3.611	–3.410	2	–4.099**
Mumbai	–4.317**	–3.995	3	–
Mormugao	–3.465	–3.382	1	–4.202**
New Mangalore	–3.762	–3.382	1	–4.176**
Cochin	–3.551	–3.410	2	–4.343**
Tuticorin	–3.570	–3.446	3	–4.288**
Chennai	–3.566	–3.446	3	–4.187**
Vizag	–4.748**	–3.995	3	–
Paradip	–3.501	–3.446	3	–4.002**
Kolkata	–3.494	–3.446	3	–4.122**
Haldia	–3.872	–3.446	3	–4.154**

Notes: 1. ADF at level. 2. MacKinnon critical values (MCV) for rejection of hypothesis of a unit root. Value refers to same order of significance level of corresponding ADF statistic. 3. Lagged differences (LD) of independent variables. 4. At First Difference. 5. Statistics with *, ** and *** indicate rejection of null hypothesis at the 10%, 5% and 1% confidence level. 6. When the null hypothesis is rejected no differencing is required to obtain stationary data. 7. Equation considered both trend and intercept terms at level.

Based on this battery of stationarity tests, it would appear that cointegration analysis is appropriate in all cases except Mumbai and Vizag.

3.4.2 Cointegration Tests

For ports with non-stationary data, the next stage of the testing procedure is sought to detect whether there is a common stochastic trend for the data series involved.[4] Johansen and Jesulius (1990) method is applied to compute values for the trace statistics. If these values are significant, a common stochastic trend among the variables exists and the series are cointegrated. This implies that the existence of a long-run equilibrium relationship between the variables be tested. If the variables are cointegrated then an error correction term must be included as an explanatory variable in any subsequent causality test. The error correction term will represent an error term obtained from the estimated long run relationship between variables.

This cointegration tests for the two variables are shown in Table 3.2. Test statistics show the existence of a cointegrating vector across the two variables (PPI and traffic) in 11 ports of India. The statistics in the first column test the null hypothesis that there are no cointegrating vectors, N=0, against the alternative hypothesis that there exists one cointegrating vector, A=1. The second column tests one conintegrating

4 An alternative widely test is the cointegrating regression Durbin-Watson (CRDW) proposed by Sargan and Bharagava (1983), provide a table of critical values. This is performed simply by regressing Y, the variable of interest, on a constant C. If Y is random walk then disturbance, e, will have a unit root. The null hypothesis that e has a unit root is tested against the alternative that it follows a stationary first order Markov process, using the conventional DW statistic. However, the power of these tests to discriminate between unit roots and borderline-stationary processes is weak (Banerjee et al., 1993) and the small sample properties are poor. They also start from single equation OLS basis. Hence, as an alternative test, which is more powerful and not based on regression residuals, has been proposed by Johansen. The Johansen Maximum Likelihood estimation method (Johansen, 1988 and 1995; Johansen and Juselius, 1990) is based on the estimation of all the cointegrating vectors.

Table 3.2. Results of Cointegration Test

Ports		NR = 0 AR = 1	NR = 1 AR = 2
Critical Value	(5%)	19.96	9.24
Critical Value	(1%)	24.60	12.97
Kandla		23.31	3.35
Mumbai		24.93	3.49
Mormugao		16.82	1.69
New Mangalore		12.20	1.74
Cochin		22.49	2.26
Tuticorin		16.57	5.84
Chennai		20.00	5.08
Vizag		14.15	3.61
Paradip		24.73	7.71
Kolkata		23.24	7.15
Haldia		31.23	9.01

Notes: 1. The statistics in the first column test the null hypothesis that there are no cointegrating vectors, N=0, against the alternative hypothesis that there exists one cointegrating vector, A=1. The second column tests one conintegrating vector, N=1, against two cointegrating vectors, A=2, and so on. 2. Critical values for the trace statistic (at 5% and 1% level) reported by Osterwald-Lenum (1992), not those tabulated in Johansen and Juselius (1990). 3. When the test statistic exceeds the table value, the null hypothesis is rejected.

vector, N=1, against two cointegrating vectors, A=2, and so on. Each row reports the trace statistic for each port. For comparison, critical values corresponding to each column are presented at the head of Table 3.2. Note that we have taken critical values for the trace statistic (at 5 percent and 1 percent level) reported by Osterwald-Lenum (1992), not those tabulated in Johansen and Juselius (1990). When the test statistic exceeds the table value, the null hypothesis is rejected. Column 1 of Table 3.2 shows that null hypothesis is rejected for seven and three ports at 5 percent and 1 percent significance level respectively thereby indicating the presence of one cointegrating vectors across the data series. However, test statistics of all the ports fail to reject the null hypothesis in the second column. Hence, there is presence of one cointegrating vector among the variables.

The foregoing cointegration test clearly ascertains the need for inclusion of an error correction term in the causality tests. This term represents an error obtained from a model representing the relationship among the variables, and is considered a measure of the long relationship among levels of the variables. Coefficients of this model also represent a cointegrating vector. In most cases the number of cointegrating vectors is greater than zero but less than the number of variables. This indicates that subsequent causality test statistics should be viewed as the best available approximation to the true statistic.[5]

3.4.3 Granger Causality Tests

Cointegration says nothing about the direction of the causal relationship between the variables, but if two variables are found to be cointegrated, it follows that there must be Granger causality in at least one direction. The Granger (1969) approach to the question of whether X causes Y is to see how much of the current Y can be explained by past values of Y and then to see whether adding lagged values of X can improve the explanation. Y is said to be Granger-caused by X if X helps in the prediction of Y, or equivalently if the coefficients on the lagged X's are statistically significant. Note that two-way simultaneous causation is frequently the case; X Granger causes Y and Y Granger causes X.[6] To test whether X causes Y, parameters of the equation are estimated and the causality test determines if the β_j's are jointly different from zero.

5 It has been argued that while cointegrating measures long-run relationships among variables, causality applies to short-run relationships (Marin, 1992). We make no such claim. While evidence favouring cointegration can influence the method of testing for causality between variables, this evidence is not informative about their causal relationship.

6 It is important to note that the statement 'X Granger causes Y' does not imply that Y is the effect or the result of X. Granger causality measures precedence and information content but does not by itself indicate causality in the more common use of the term.

$$Y_t = \sum_{j=1}^{m} \alpha_j Y_{t-j} + \sum_{i=1}^{m} \beta_i X_{t-i} + e_t \qquad (3.3)$$

This standard Granger causality test is performed for cases where the variables are not cointegrated and also the corresponding data series are stationary. When the two variables are cointegrated, an error correction term, representing the error term from the non-differenced cointegrated relationship, be included in the equations. The reported F-statistics are the Wald statistics for the joint hypothesis.

$$\beta_1 = \ldots\ldots\ldots = \beta_j = 0$$

for each equation. The null hypothesis is therefore that X does not Granger-cause Y in the first regression and that Y does not Granger-cause X in the second regression.

Hence, causality is tested by specifying two equations similar to equation (3.3) on two variables namely port performance and port traffic for all the 11 ports. Thus the equations may be rewritten as

$$\Delta PPI_t = \sum_{j=1}^{m} \alpha_j \Delta PPI_{t-j} + \sum_{i=1}^{m} \beta_i \Delta Traffic_{t-i} + u_t \qquad (3.4)$$

$$\Delta Traffic_t = \sum_{j=1}^{m} \delta_j \Delta Traffic_{t-j} + \sum_{i=1}^{m} \varphi_i \Delta PPI_{t-i} + v_t \qquad (3.5)$$

For there to be unidirectional causality from traffic to PPI, the estimated coefficients on lagged traffic in equation (3.4) should be significantly different from zero as a group ($\Sigma\beta_i \neq 0$) and the set of estimated coefficients on lagged PPI ($\Sigma\varphi_i$) in the second equation should not be significantly different from zero. Bilateral causality (or, what may be called as simultaneity) is suggested when both $\Sigma\beta_i \neq 0$ in (3.4) and $\Sigma\varphi_i \neq 0$ in (3.5) and independent when both sets of coefficients are not significantly different from zero.

Results of the causality tests are given in Table 3.3. Test was performed considering one and two years lag for all the ports involving both 'without error correction term' and 'with error correction term'. Although one test is applicable for each port, performing both types of tests is useful for comparison. At 5 percent confidence level, the relatively larger ports like Kandla, Mumbai, Chennai, Vizag support the hypothesis that performance causes traffic. Using a more liberal 10 percent confidence level, Tuticorin is also consistent with the causality from performance to traffic hypothesis. When an error correction term is included, causality between performance and traffic in Cochin becomes significant at 5 percent confidence level. Table 3.4 represents the above results briefly. Evidence from this cointegration tests indicate that these results may be slightly biased. Even taking this bias into consideration, these results clearly imply that efforts to adopt performance augmenting technologies or performance improvement measurements will have some positive influence on port traffic.

While more ports provide evidence in favour of the performance causes traffic hypothesis, only one port confirms the simultaneous relationship that is Haldia, which is an estuarine port located in the eastern part of the country. This may be due to the fact that the port of Haldia is served by a larger hinterland; it has rather a mixed industrial feedback generated from the very industrial township of Haldia and captive bulk cargo. Interestingly, no port confirms the reverse hypothesis, i.e. traffic causes performance. Even inclusion of an error correction term fails to reverse the general outcomes. No significant relationship has been found in case of New Mangalore, Mormugao and Paradip. These are the ports which are specially equipped to handle bulk cargo, either bulk solid and bulk liquid and focus less on performance augmenting factors due to static captive demand/supply of traffic in overseas and/or local markets. Moreover, these ports serve largely local and well-defined hinterlands and face little competition. Finally, the role of these ports in Indian total port traffic has not been significant over last two decades.

The results from this chapter demonstrate that even in the presence of cointegration among a set of variables, inclusion of an error correction term in the Granger test has little empirically observable effect on the results. It may be concluded that to attain higher traffic, ports obviously should give highest priority to their performance by improving operational performance factors like PBWT, TRT, and asset performance indicators like BOR, BTR. These four most important determinants of port performance as appeared in the post-liberalisation period from principal component analysis are related to the degree of port congestion.

Table 3.3. Granger Causality Test

Ports	Null Hypothesis	W/O EC F-Statistic	With EC F-Statistic	W/O EC F-Statistic	With EC F-Statistic
	Number of lags	1	1	2	2
	Critical value (at 5%)	3.71	3.71	3.84	3.84
	Critical value (at 1%)	6.55	6.55	7.01	7.01
Kandla	Traffic does not Cause Performance	7.089***	7.934***	3.986**	4.054**
	Performance does not Cause Traffic	0.565	0.588	0.957	1.320
Mumbai	Traffic does not Cause Performance	8.712***	8.933***	4.167**	4.342**
	Performance does not Cause Traffic	0.022	0.176	1.885	1.944
Mormugao	Traffic does not Cause Performance	0.002	0.003	0.045	0.034
	Performance does not Cause Traffic	0.068	0.189	0.337	0.672
New Mangalore	Traffic does not Cause Performance	0.650	0.744	0.162	0.203
	Performance does not Cause Traffic	1.160	1.452	0.361	0.388
Cochin	Traffic does not Cause Performance	2.112	2.542	4.340**	4.986**
	Performance does not Cause Traffic	0.312	0.567	0.206	0.332
Tuticorin	Traffic does not Cause Performance	3.584*	3.664*	1.458	1.893
	Performance does not Cause Traffic	0.023	0.099	0.030	0.098
Chennai	Traffic does not Cause Performance	10.491***	13.452***	5.488**	6.554**
	Performance does not Cause Traffic	0.236	0.398	0.294	0.302
Vizag	Traffic does not Cause Performance	4.097**	4.002**	1.321	1.340
	Performance does not Cause Traffic	0.207	0.205	0.132	0.198
Paradip	Traffic does not Cause Performance	2.604	2.675	1.629	1.657
	Performance does not Cause Traffic	0.001	0.001	0.697	0.762
Kolkata	Traffic does not Cause Performance	5.735**	6.670***	3.114	3.965**
	Performance does not Cause Traffic	0.301	0.430	1.301	1.340
Haldia	Traffic does not Cause Performance	3.474*	4.330**	3.967**	4.872**
	Performance does not Cause Traffic	3.385*	5.340**	1.593	1.672

Notes: 1. The reported F-statistics are the Wald statistics for the joint hypothesis. 2. W/O EC and With EC mean Without error correction terms and With error correction terms respectively. 3. Cause means 'Granger Cause'. 4. Statistics with *, ** and *** indicate rejection of null hypothesis at the 10%, 5% and 1% confidence level. 5. Significance of a variable demonstrates causality.

Table 3.4. Direction of Causal Relationship

Ports	Causal Relationship
Kandla	Performance → Traffic
Mumbai	Performance → Traffic
Mormugao	*
New Mangalore	*
Cochin	Performance → Traffic[1]
Tuticorin	Performance → Traffic[1]
Chennai	Performance → Traffic
Vizag	Performance → Traffic
Paradip	*
Kolkata	Performance → Traffic
Haldia	Performance ↔ Traffic[2]

Notes: 1. Weak relation. 2. Simultaneous relation. *No causal relationship found.

Hence, for attracting higher traffic, policy towards performance augmenting facilities shall be given priority so that higher efficiency induces higher traffic.

3.5 Conclusions

The major finding of this chapter is that in no port does traffic cause performance and most of the ports provide evidence towards the fact that performance causes traffic in India. Hence, it should not be surprising that performance does lead to increased traffic in a liberal economic regime. This chapter uses some individual port performance indicators, which are largely internal to each of the ports, for finding causal relationship with port traffic. If a port performs better by improving its operational and asset performance then it is likely to get higher traffic.

Policies to increase efficiency have been pursued in port sector in many countries by changing the structure and institutional framework of this industry. The changes have been introduced across the globe by such measures as privatisation and deregulation so that the role of governments has been reduced significantly. The countries in which the policy changes have been greatest are those in which national policies exerted a strong influence on port performance. The more competitive environment has implications for national port policies and for port management. Indian government has taken some discrete initiatives in recent period for expanding the country's port capacity. But no comprehensive policy has yet been announced for augmenting port performance. The improvement of operational performance of Indian ports has been a priority policy objective for many years, but notwithstanding the vast technical assistance provided by international organisations and various countries, the results have often been disappointing. According to the Government of India (2007), approximately US$ 18 billion is required to invest by 2011–12 to provide adequate port facility in this country. Realising the urgent need for inter- and intra- port competition to attain higher performance level, the Government of India has invited the private sector to finance new port facilities. Although success to date is not unsatisfactory, substantial improvement will remain out of reach until a fundamental restructuring and changes in management culture are implemented, which will take a considerable time to achieve. Hence, there is an urgent need for a comprehensive policy, which will strongly influence on port performance and will be consistent with the globalisation programme.

Questions may also be raised as to the usefulness of port performance index derived from principal component analysis. Notwithstanding the specific roles played by various individual port performance indicators, it can not be denied that some judicious combinations of these factors lead to perfect coordination for maximising over all port efficiency. At there is no other rationale method for doing so; we can not but use the indexation method described in this chapter. Above all such weighting mechanism will help the policy makers to strengthen the weaker factors for improving the overall performance index.

The limitations of this study are briefed below. First, we have not considered here the spatial concentration of manufacturing activities in and around the ports, differential geographical attributes, logistics networks, and differential nation-wide infrastructure stocks associated with each region, which may have very substantial bearings on port traffic. The findings of this study may be further substantiated incorporating these exogenous factors. Second, implication of this study might have been stronger if some external factors which have direct bearings on port traffic and performance like depth of the navigational channel, nature of shipping routes and vessel sizes, level of technologically advanced equipment, etc. were considered. Third, given the aggregate nature of the performance index, there is some potential for obtaining biased results. Fourth, Granger causality test considers long time period properties. For this reason, conclusions obtained in this chapter are subject to revision if conducted by tests based on a larger period.

Future work can attempt to measure causal relationship between cargo-specific performance and traffic for each port and then perform the procedures described in this book. The reason for this is that most of the Indian ports are designed to handle specific categories of cargo, which have declined over time while other types of traffic have gained importance. But the port's berth configurations have not yet adjusted to the new categories of cargo. In this backdrop, such an analysis can lead to distinct results for each cargo baskets in each port. Having analysed the causal relationship between traffic and performance in Indian port sector, it would also be appropriate to assess the total factor productivity growth of Indian ports giving special emphasis on post-1991 liberalisation programme. This has been dealt with in the next chapter.

Appendix 3.1 Results of Unit Root: Phillips–Perron (PP) Test

(a) Port Performance

Ports	PP	MCV[1]	LD[2]
Kandla	–5.365***	–4.887	1
Mumbai	–4.975***	–4.887	2
Mormugao	–3.402*	–3.359	2
New Mangalore	–3.429*	–3.359	2
Cochin	–3.386*	–3.359	2
Tuticorin	–3.412*	–3.359	2
Chennai	–4.818**	–3.829	2
Vizag	–4.568**	–3.829	2
Paradip	–3.573*	–3.359	2
Kolkata	–3.368*	–3.359	2
Haldia	–4.766**	–3.829	2

(b) Port Traffic

Ports	PP	MCV[1]	LD[2]
Kandla	–3.622	–3.359	2
Mumbai	–3.362*	–3.359	2
Mormugao	–3.811*	–3.359	2
New Mangalore	–3.662	–3.359	2
Cochin	–3.438	–3.359	2
Tuticorin	–3.621	–3.359	2
Chennai	–3.419	–3.359	2
Vizag	–3.385*	–3.359	2
Paradip	–5.540***	–4.887	2
Kolkata	–3.369	–3.359	2
Haldia	–3.693*	–3.359	2

Notes: 1. MacKinnon critical values (MCV) for rejection of hypothesis of a unit root. Value refers to same order of significance level of corresponding PP statistic. 2. Lagged differences (LD) of independent variables. Here lag truncation for Bartlett kernel taken at two years period for most of the pairs except Kandla. 3. Statistics with *, ** and *** indicate rejection of null hypothesis at the 10%, 5% and 1% confidence level. 4. When the null hypothesis is rejected no differencing is required to obtain stationary data. 5. Equation considered both trend and intercept terms at level. 8. Data were taken at logarithms form.

Total Factor Productivity Growth in Ports

4.1 Introduction

Globalisation has led to the increasing importance of performance of port. Productivity and efficiency are the two important concepts in measuring performance. Over the last decade or so, these two similar but different concepts have been used interchangeably by various scholars (Coelli et al., 1998). The present chapter aims to assess total factor productivity (TFP) growth of Indian port sector.

Recent trends in international trade have led to the increasing importance of port as prime mode of transportation. Standing at the interface of sea and inland transportation, ports play a pivotal role in the merchandise transportation process. Modern ports need a significant amount of investment in order to develop and maintain both their infrastructure and superstructure. At the same time, however, modern logistics and hub-and-spoke transportation patterns have meant that ports face much fiercer competition than ever before (Cullinane and Khanna, 2000; Reveley and Tull, 2008). As such, modern container ports suffer from both internal and external pressure. On the one hand, they need to exhibit management competency in the pursuit of a suitable strategy and in the allocation of scarce resources. On the other, many container ports can no longer enjoy the freedom yielded by a monopoly over handling of cargoes within their hinterland. Thus, performance measurement is the normal way to handle internal and external pressures, by monitoring and benchmarking a port's production.

It is under the above backdrop, our objective in this chapter is to assess total factor productivity (TFP) growth of Indian port sector with particular emphasis on India's liberalisation programmes. Section 4.2 focuses on productivity and efficiency concepts. TFP model and the sources of data are briefed in Section 4.3. Section 4.4 is devoted to empirical results, and, finally, summary and conclusions are drawn in Section 4.5.

4.2 Productivity and Efficiency Concepts

Production, which can be simply defined as a process by which inputs are combined, transformed and turned into outputs (Case and Fair, 1999), is a fundamental concept in economic theory. The inputs can normally be generalised as natural resources such as land, human resources and man-made aids to further production (like tools and machinery). Outputs, on the other hand, can be categorised into tangible products including goods and intangible products including services. Studying production is of great significance because of scarce resources and the human desire to fully utilise them.

Productivity and efficiency are the two most important but different concepts in measuring performance. The productivity of a producer can be loosely defined as the ratio of output(s) to input(s). This definition is easily and very obviously capable of explaining any situation where there is a single output and single input. As production has multiple outputs and inputs, it is more common to refer to TFP; a productivity measure involving all factors of production (Coelli et al., 1998).

Efficiency can be defined as relative productivity over time or space, or both. For instance, it can be divided into intra- and inter-firm efficiency measures. The former involves measuring the use of the firm's own production potential by computing the productivity level over time relative to a firm-specific Production Frontier, which refers to the set of maximum outputs given the different level of inputs. In contrast, the latter measures the performance of a particular firm relative to its best counterpart(s) available in the industry (Lansink et al., 2001).

The difference between efficiency and productivity is illustrated in Figure 4.1. Points A, B and C refer to three different producers. The productivity of point A can be measured by the ratio AD/OD according

Figure 4.1. Illustration of Efficiency and Productivity

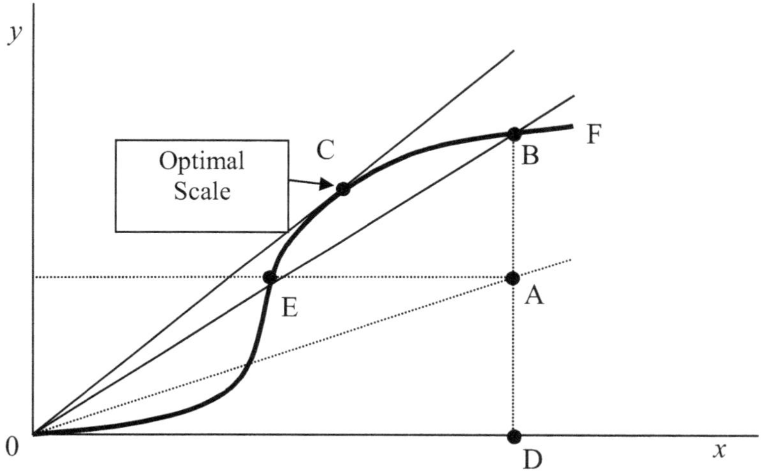

Source: Derived from Coelli et al. (1998)

to the definition of productivity where the x-axis represents inputs and the y-axis denotes outputs.

Given the same input, it is quite clear that productivity can be further improved by moving from point A to point B. The new level of productivity is then given by BD/OD. Clearly, productivity can be represented, therefore, by the slope of the ray through the origin which joins the specific point under study. The efficiency of point A, on the other hand, can be measured as follows by the ratio of the productivity of point A to that of point B.

$$\frac{AD / OD}{BD / OD}$$

The above efficiency is normally termed Technical Efficiency, and includes output- and input-oriented technical efficiencies, i.e., the producer can either improve output given the same input (output-oriented, point A to B) or reduce the input given the same output (input-oriented, point A to E) by improving technology.

The heavy curve OF in Figure 4.1 is the so-called production frontier. All the points on the production frontier are technically efficient, whilst all the points below or lying to the right of the efficient frontier are technically inefficient. The production frontier reflects the current state of technology in the industry.

The ray through the origin and point C in Figure 4.1 is at a tangent to the production frontier, and hence defines the point of maximum possible productivity. This leads to another important concept, Scale Efficiency, which relates to a possible divergence between actual and ideal production size.

Allocative efficiency is another important concept in the context of production economics. Unlike technical and scale efficiencies, which only consider physical quantities and technical relationships and do not address issues such as costs or profits, allocative efficiency studies the costs of production given that the information on prices and a behavioural assumption such as cost minimisation or profit maximisation is properly established. For instance, allocative efficiency in input selection occurs when a selection of inputs (e.g. materials, labour and capital) produce a given quantity of output at minimum cost given the prevailing input prices (Coelli et al., 1998).

To conclude, it is no easy way to designate any performance as 'good' or 'bad' unless compared to some preconceived level, or to that of another unit. It is common to describe the performance of a production unit in terms of 'more or less efficient', and 'more or less productive'. What is the basic difference between these two terms? By the productivity of a production unit one means the ratio of its output to input. Such ratio is easy to compute if the unit uses a single input to produce a single output. But the more likely event is that it uses several inputs to produce several outputs. In that case the inputs and outputs must be aggregated in some economically reasonable manner so that the productivity will be a ratio of two scalars. Productivity varies due to differences in the environment in which production occurs, differences in technology, labour and input qualities. By the efficiency of production units one means a comparison between 'observed' and 'optimal' values of its outputs and inputs, where the comparison can take the form of the ratio between observed to maximum potential output obtainable from the given inputs (which is called 'production efficiency' or 'technical efficiency'), or the ratio of minimum potential to observed input required to produce the given output (called 'cost efficiency'). But unless disaggregated, preferably firm level, data are available none of these methods will be very fruitful. Here we will be particularly interested in understanding productivity, namely (i) labour productivity in the sense of value added per unit of labour, and (ii) total factor productivity in the sense of 'unexplained residual' from the contributions of labour and capital.

4.2.1 The TFP Model

The TFP is a measure of technological change in industry. It is indeed a very old concept in the classical literature of economic growth and development. It can be expressed as a ration between real product and real factor inputs used in the production process. Strictly speaking, it was first introduced and used by Jan Tinbergen way back in 1942 in paper written in German which was not translated into English until 1959. Hence, the popular belief traces back its origin to Solow's (1957) influential empirical work on US economy. But quite a large number of studies can be found using this concept of technological development even before Solow (1957). Among these, Johnson (1950), Schmookler (1952), Kendrick (1956), Abramovitz (1956), Rutton (1956) are important.[1] While these and a significant number of studies after them have often focused on the non-frontier approach of calculating TFP growth, the frontier approach to TFP measurement was first initiated by Farrell (1957) but it was not until the late 1970s that this approach was formalised and used for empirical investigation (Mahadevan, 2004). The flow chart in Figure 4.2 is used to map out the main TFP measuring methods under the frontier and non-frontier approach.

1 For a critical review, see Nadiri (1970, 1972), Kennedy and Thirlwall (1972), Nelson (1981), Griliches (1996), Griliches and Jorgenson (1966), and Felipe and McCombie (2003).

Figure 4.2. TFP Estimation Methods

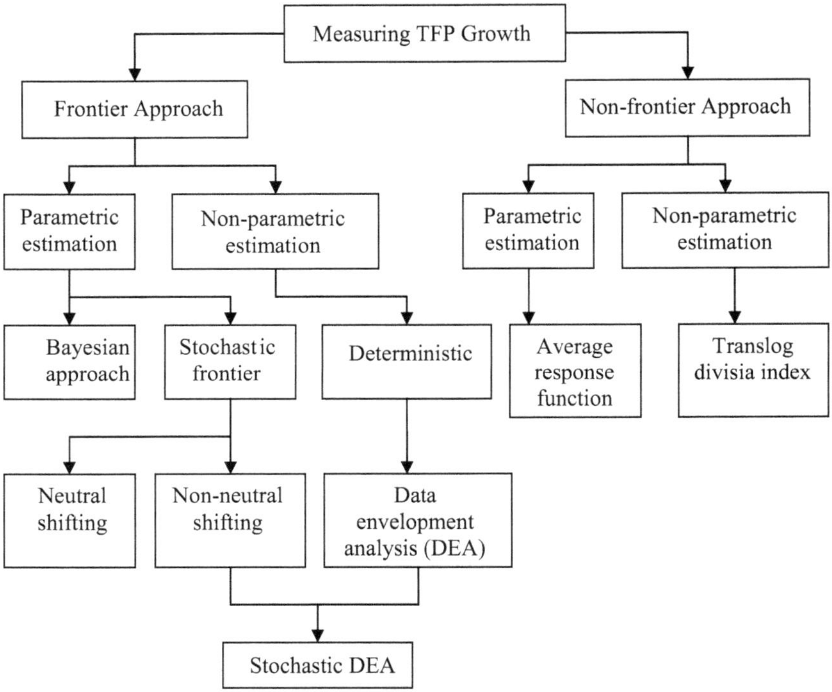

Source: Derived from Mahadevan (2004)

There are two related approaches to the measurement of TFP: the production function approach and the growth accounting approach using some fixed shares. In our study, we use the first approach explicitly in terms of a Cobb-Douglas production function. The econometric approach to estimation of TFP demands that we must specify the form of the function. In a single commodity two factor world, it looks like

$$Y_t = A_t L_t^{\alpha} K_t^{(1-\alpha)} \tag{4.1}$$

where Y_t, L_t and K_t are output (in our case port traffic), labour input and capital input used in the production process at time t respectively. A_t is the technology parameter which conceals within it all the myths about the invisible that governs the shift in production function. Here α

is the output elasticity of labour, (1-α) is that of capital, and the sum of these two elasticities is one, which simply means constant returns to scale. The form of A_t can be defined in many ways, but we consider the simplest one i.e. equation (4.2).

$$A_t = A_0 e^{\lambda t} \quad (4.2)$$

The equation (4.2) implies that technology progresses at a constant exponential rate of λ. Putting this value into (4.1), we get

$$Y_t = A_0 e^{\lambda t} L_t^{\alpha} K_t^{(1-\alpha)} \quad (4.3)$$

Taking logarithm on both sides gives us the final estimable equation.

$$LnY_t = LnA_0 + \lambda t + \alpha\, LnL_t + (1-\alpha)K_t \quad (4.4)$$

To derive the TFP estimates in our particular case, we incorporate time coefficients into the equation (4.4), and we get

$$LnY_t = Ln\, A_0 + \lambda\, t + \alpha\, Ln\, L_t + (1-\alpha)\, Ln\, K_t + D_1\, t_1 \quad (4.5)$$

$$LnY_t = Ln\, A_0 + \lambda\, t + \alpha\, Ln\, L_t + (1-\alpha)\, Ln\, K_t + D_1\, t_1 + D_2\, t_2 \quad (4.6)$$

where time dummy in equation (4.5) is for the whole period (1980–81 to 2005–06), and the additional time dummy in equation (4.6) is for the period 1991–92 to 2005–06. Purpose of putting an additional dummy in equation (4.6) is basically to test the impact of economic reforms initiated in India in 1991.

What is important is that equation (4.4) helps us to estimate the technology parameter (λ), the labour elasticity (α) and the capital elasticity (1-α) if we have the time series data on Y, K and L. The determination of λ helps to understand the contribution of technological change to the growth of output in the Indian port sector. However, the meaning of λ must be clearly understood before extending it too far as is very common in the existing literature. λ is disembodied, exogenous and Hicks-neutral technological progress. 'Disembodied' technological change means that it is not embodied into the factor inputs (labour and/or capital) but it takes place like 'manna from heaven' in the forms of better methods, organisation and management of production that improve efficiency of input use. 'Exogenous' here means that it is independent of the variables utilised in the growth model. Therefore, we are left only with 'time' as the only factor. Quite contrary to this, the entire endogenous growth literature has been based on various internal (in a sense man-made) factors of production which govern or which have strong influence on productivity, efficiency and technological change. According to this literature, the important factors are education, R&D investment, experience, various forms of infrastructure facilities and the like (Krugman, 1979; Romer, 1986; Aschauer, 1989; Barro and Sala-i-Martin, 1995).

One special feature of this Hicks-neutral technical change is that it has the uniform effect of increasing the efficiency on both labor and capital, whereas Harrod-neutral one is labor-augmenting and Solow-neutral is capital-augmenting. Given these distinctions, the meaning of λ should be interpreted very cautiously. For all practical purposes, there may be situations when λ may appear to be small, but that should not be taken to mean that 'embodied' technological progress is also small; in fact, quite reverse may be the case; moreover, λ may be small due to misspecification of production function, failure to take into account both public and private infrastructure capital (that is exogenous factors), inappropriate policy mix, and the like. On the other hand, a large λ may be the outcome of monopoly factor and related economies of scale, and other unknown factors. On the whole, this λ fails to take into account the entire range of external factors on which port has no direct control and social, economic and political infrastructure facilities like education, transport, R&D, energy, openness, governance, and the like.

There is another methodology for estimating TFP change. This second method is strictly contingent upon the assumption of constant factor shares. For example, in this growth accounting approach, shares of labour and capital in national income are assumed to remain constant and these are used as weights for estimating the 'residual' in productivity growth that can not be explained by mere inputs growth. This TFP is by analogy therefore the same as our technology parameter (λ): the same disembodied, exogenous and Hicks-neutral technological change. This method has one advantage. It can be fruitfully used for cases where data for only terminal years are available. But that too is a heroic assumption as it is too much sensitive to extreme observations. The reader should bear in mind that neither method is full-proof. But in the ultimate reality, there is adequate evidence to prove that factor shares remain hardly constant even over the medium time series of more than a decade; this is more so for any developing country like India; and even for Japan and USA, there is always a changing composition of factor shares (Kuznets, 1955; Hicks, 1932). It is also very persuasive to mention that TFP as calculated from the factor share model is a mere 'residual', a left out value as an error term that cannot be explained by increases in factor inputs. As rightly remarked by Abramovitz (1956), it is simply an 'index of our ignorance'. We, however, refrain from discussing the growth accounting approach as we are not going to deal with it here. Chronologically, studies on TFP came to a halt in the Western world from the late 1970s. Economists there became more and more interested in the detailed breakdown of the inputs in terms of quality considerations, R&D, education, infrastructure facilities. The recent resurgence in the renewed interest in such an outdated technique may have been possible by the recent studies of the Young (1994, 1995), and Krugman (1994a, 1994b).

4.2.2 Data

In view of aforesaid discussion, we have chosen the period of our analysis is 1980–81 to 2005–06. A period of 26 years is supposed to be reasonable enough for our purpose to check the extent of the impact of new technology on the productivity of the factors of production in Indian port sector. However, technological issues like import of technical know-how and/or techniques are basically embodied in our analysis and not directly dealt with.

It may be admitted here that the measurement of the stock of capital always poses some conceptual problems. For our purpose, we have followed the Perpetual Inventory Accumulation (PIA) method. Most researchers who have dealt with capital stock in Indian industries (and also elsewhere) have preferred to use the gross fixed capital stock (GFCS), perpetuated from the base year and converted into real terms with the help of capital formation deflators. In fact, there are conflicting views about the measurement of capital in general, and that in Indian industry particular. One basic and pioneering work on capital stock

Table 4.1. Growth Rates of Input and Output in Indian Ports

(%)

Ports	Years	Y	Y/L	K/L
Kandla	1980–81 – 2005–06	17.00	19.93	0.69
	1980–81 – 1990–91	12.48	11.68	–3.47
	1990–91 – 2005–06	9.24	12.37	6.35
Mumbai	1980–81 – 2005–06	3.47	7.89	13.56
	1980–81 – 1990–91	7.02	9.19	0.34
	1990–91 – 2005–06	0.31	3.55	23.77
Jawaharlal Nehru	1989–90 – 2005–06	334.95	202.58	–3.98
	1990–91 – 2005–06	136.33	99.75	13.24
Mormugao	1980–81 – 2005–06	4.66	4.72	0.14
	1980–81 – 1990–91	0.84	0.02	–4.25
	1990–91 – 2005–06	7.24	8.62	6.60
New Mangalore	1980–81 – 2005–06	121.73	70.14	–0.22
	1980–81 – 1990–91	73.54	64.86	–4.17
	1990–91 – 2005–06	19.38	9.96	5.26
Cochin	1980–81 – 2005–06	7.25	15.66	18.66
	1980–81 – 1990–91	3.92	6.18	10.39
	1990–91 – 2005–06	7.20	14.56	12.53
Tuticorin	1980–81 – 2005–06	19.74	16.06	2.12
	1980–81 – 1990–91	9.84	11.33	–3.35
	1990–91 – 2005–06	14.11	9.38	10.04
Chennai	1980–81 – 2005–06	11.53	14.89	11.27
	1980–81 – 1990–91	13.62	15.70	0.44
	1990–91 – 2005–06	4.14	5.53	19.43
Vizag	1980–81 – 2005–06	16.90	41.98	8.42
	1980–81 – 1990–91	9.19	13.03	–1.29
	1990–91 – 2005–06	12.15	28.70	18.96
Paradip	1980–81 – 2005–06	46.81	92.18	14.11
	1980–81 – 1990–91	20.71	28.27	–1.96
	1990–91 – 2005–06	22.32	38.00	34.23
Haldia	1980–81 – 2005–06	22.49	13.73	–2.05
	1980–81 – 1990–91	10.42	6.13	–5.41
	1990–91 – 2005–06	15.94	12.44	1.64
Kolkata	1980–81 – 2005–06	5.18	29.98	5.08
	1980–81 – 1990–91	0.15	5.01	–0.57
	1990–91 – 2005–06	9.24	33.84	10.38

in Indian industries is Hashim and Dadi (1973). Some of the other important works using this method are Roychoudhury (1977) and Ahluwalia (1991). We have estimated the GFCS, taking 1951–52 (the beginning of the 1st Five Year Plan) as the base year.

The major source of our data relating to traffic and labour of Indian ports is various issues of Basic Port Statistics of India, published by the Ministry of Shipping, Highways and Road Transport, Government of India. The port-wise capital was collected from the various Plan Statistics, published by the Planning Commission, Government of India. While tabulating port-wise capital, we have only considered year-wise plan expenditure rather than plan outlay except for the year 2005–06. Year-wise GFCS data were converted into real terms with the help of capital formation deflator (base 1993–94 = 100), obtained from the National Accounts Statistics, Government of India.

4.3 Empirical Results on TFP Changes

4.3.1 Relative Growth Rates of Output and Input

The annual growth rates of Y, K/L, and Y/L of India's major ports are presented in Table 4.1. To capture the impact of liberalisation in the growth process, we have divided the entire period of our study into the three parts: 1980–81 to 2005–06, 1980–81 to 1990–91, and 1990–91 to 2005–06. Some important observations are worth noting.

First, except Chennai, rest major ports located in the east coast have recorded higher growth rates in traffic during the post-liberalisation period (1990–91 to 2005–06) than that of pre-liberalisation period (1980–81 to 1990–91). In case of major ports located on the west coast, except Cochin and Mormugao, growth of traffic for rest major ports was decelerated in the post-liberalisation period.

Second, in case of labour productivity (LP), we have seen mixed results. In the post-liberalisation period, Mumbai, New Mangalore,

Table 4.2. Estimation of TFP Growth through Cobb-Douglas Production Function: 1980–81 to 2005–06

Port	Independent Variables	Coefficients	t-stat	Adj R^2	F value	SEE	DW	SC
Kandla	Intercept	26.7495	3.3249	0.9493	18.42	0.0274	1.8943	0.2785
	Ln(K)	–0.2655	–1.4777					
	Ln(L)	–0.5617	–0.9924					
	TFP1	0.0622	10.1566					
Kandla	Intercept	26.9249	3.2806	0.9474	19.984	0.0795	1.9130	0.2823
	Ln(K)	–0.2916	–1.5385					
	Ln(L)	–0.5158	–0.8842					
	TFP1	0.0657	7.1779					
	TFP2	–0.0551	–0.5348					
Mumbai	Intercept	23.0593	6.6936	0.6938	17.613	0.09181	1.1159	0.2966
	Ln(K)	–0.3712	–3.5234					
	Ln(L)	0.1822	0.9399					
	TFP1	0.0322	6.9223					
Mumbai	Intercept	23.8598	7.2811	0.7278	15.706	0.08656	1.1800	0.2924
	Ln(K)	–0.4232	–4.0979					
	Ln(L)	0.2101	1.1454					
	TFP1	0.0434	5.7754					
	TFP2	–0.1399	–1.8375					
Jawaharlal Nehru	Intercept	19.2657	0.4326	0.9651	120.34	0.19712	1.6750	–0.0333
	Ln(K)	–0.5339	–0.3367					
	Ln(L)	0.9782	0.7755					
	TFP1	0.2084	8.8395					

Table 4.2 continued

Table 4.2 continued

Port	Independent Variables	Coefficients	t-stat	Adj R^2	F value	SEE	DW	SC
Jawaharlal Nehru	Intercept	10.3261	0.2097	0.9622	83.814	0.20464	1.8597	–0.1159
	Ln(K)	–0.1044	–0.0569					
	Ln(L)	0.8286	0.6185					
	TFP1	0.2107	8.4768					
	TFP2	0.1784	0.5278					
Mormugao	Intercept	15.6939	5.9172	0.8633	47.321	0.07151	1.9258	0.0299
	Ln(K)	0.2864	3.2435					
	Ln(L)	–0.6775	–3.1632					
	TFP1	0.0292	11.9014					
Mormugao	Intercept	14.9223	5.0103	0.8587	34.413	0.07272	1.9819	–0.0034
	Ln(K)	0.3079	3.1930					
	Ln(L)	–0.6383	–2.8112					
	TFP1	0.0266	5.3906					
	TFP2	0.0411	0.6108					
New Mangalore	Intercept	29.0705	6.5401	0.9372	40.41	0.20786	1.9747	0.3515
	Ln(K)	–0.5323	–2.4194					
	Ln(L)	–0.4797	–1.5116					
	TFP1	0.1456	11.7400					
New Mangalore	Intercept	29.3812	8.6777	0.9636	146.5	0.15829	1.5561	0.0535
	Ln(K)	–0.7293	–4.1624					
	Ln(L)	0.0559	0.2005					
	TFP1	0.1696	14.9812					
	TFP2	–0.5890	–3.8425					

Table 4.2 continued

Table 4.2 continued

Port	Independent Variables	Coefficients	t-stat	Adj R^2	F value	SEE	DW	SC
Cochin	Intercept	30.9014	4.1741	0.9038	69.905	0.11353	1.5881	0.1991
	Ln(K)	–0.6577	–2.3183					
	Ln(L)	–0.1966	–0.5809					
	TFP1	0.0670	6.9523					
Cochin	Intercept	31.6360	4.1289	0.9001	50.57	0.11568	1.6434	0.1720
	Ln(K)	–0.6927	–2.3396					
	Ln(L)	–0.1977	–0.5735					
	TFP1	0.0715	5.5575					
	TFP2	–0.0542	–0.5471					
Tuticorin	Intercept	15.1424	13.7845	0.9841	450.79	0.06477	1.4429	0.2699
	Ln(K)	–0.0204	–0.4244					
	Ln(L)	0.0017	0.0140					
	TFP1	0.0752	31.6625					
Tuticorin	Intercept	15.1692	12.6141	0.9831	320.38	0.06653	1.4484	0.2677
	Ln(K)	–0.0212	–0.4157					
	Ln(L)	0.0004	0.0034					
	TFP1	0.0755	16.0986					
	TFP2	–0.0038	–0.0645					
Chennai	Intercept	1.5312	0.1431	0.8966	64.594	0.12819	2.2387	–0.1300
	Ln(K)	–0.5380	–4.5191					
	Ln(L)	2.8138	2.2754					
	TFP1	0.1026	6.5000					

Table 4.2 continued

Table 4.2 continued

Port	Independent Variables	Coefficients	t-stat	Adj R^2	F value	SEE	DW	SC
Chennai	Intercept	13.8039	1.0692	0.9041	52.865	0.12345	2.4345	–0.2232
	Ln(K)	–0.5686	–4.8903					
	Ln(L)	1.5773	1.1065					
	TFP	0.1052	6.8803					
	TFP2	–0.2134	–1.5777					
Vizag	Intercept	16.6800	2.2219	0.9711	247.73	0.08881	1.6623	0.1460
	Ln(K)	–0.0762	–0.3835					
	Ln(L)	0.1049	0.2890					
	TFP1	0.0793	8.2245					
Vizag	Intercept	16.2945	2.1266	0.9701	179.69	0.09033	1.7320	0.1031
	Ln(K)	–0.0799	–0.3955					
	Ln(L)	0.1527	0.4044					
	TFP1	0.0839	6.7817					
	TFP2	–0.0494	–0.6049					
Paradip	Intercept	19.4848	1.8949	0.9305	39.118	0.02159	1.7794	0.3487
	Ln(K)	–0.2335	–1.1878					
	Ln(L)	–0.0197	–0.0235					
	TFP1	0.1286	6.6520					
Paradip	Intercept	18.0818	1.7474	0.9308	34.948	0.02109	1.8527	0.3877
	Ln(K)	–0.2395	–1.2207					
	Ln(L)	0.1493	0.1756					
	TFP1	0.1461	5.7194					
	TFP2	–0.1984	–1.0423					

Table 4.2 continued

Table 4.2 continued

Port	Independent Variables	Coefficients	t-stat	Adj R^2	F value	SEE	DW	SC
Haldia	Intercept	17.5181	7.8467	0.9921	918.38	0.04644	2.0778	–0.1965
	Ln(K)	0.0589	0.8727					
	Ln(L)	–0.4267	–2.2406					
	TFP1	0.0851	21.7900					
Haldia	Intercept	17.4586	7.3312	0.9916	652.85	0.04771	2.0767	–0.1955
	Ln(K)	0.0588	0.8483					
	Ln(L)	–0.4192	–1.9795					
	TFP1	0.0853	20.2715					
	TFP2	–0.0040	–0.0926					
Kolkata	Intercept	28.7976	1.1015	0.6747	16.207	0.169	1.3146	0.3420
	Ln(K)	–0.1050	–0.1363					
	Ln(L)	–1.0891	–1.1308					
	TFP1	–0.0305	–0.4263					
Kolkata	Intercept	29.3981	1.1135	0.6685	12.089	0.1706	1.3870	0.3057
	Ln(K)	–0.1094	–0.1406					
	Ln(L)	–1.1343	–1.1648					
	TFP1	–0.0407	–0.5557					
	TFP2	0.1149	0.8030					

Note. TFP1 and TFP2 refer to equations 4.5 and 4.6 respectively.

Tuticorin and Chennai have witnessed fall in labour productivities while rest of the major ports have witnessed rise in labour productivities in the same period. The steep rise of LP in Kolkata port in the post-liberalisation period is remarkable while the drastic fall of LP in case of New Mangalore port is a matter of serious concern.

Third, one of the interesting features of this growth analysis is that average annual growth rates of Y/L for most of the major ports have significantly outweighed those of traffic.

Fourth, as indicated earlier, capital labour ratio (K/L) is defined as the amount of real GFCS per unit of labour at any point of time. Here, except Haldia, rest of the major ports have witnessed rise in K/L in the post-liberalisation period compared to that of pre-liberalisation period (Figure 4.3). The rise in K/L ratio is the result of a simultaneous increase in capital itself and decline in size of employment uniformly in all these ports except Haldia. This outcome in general indicates that Indian ports have been witnessing infusion of more capital as well as fall in employment in the post-liberalisation period, which, in other words, indicates Indian ports are becoming more capital intensive in the post-liberalisation period. The rise in K/L is the result of a widespread capital deepening process in Indian port sector.

4.3.2 Changes in TFPG: 1980–81 to 2005–06

We have derived the TFP estimates from equations 4.5 and 4.6. This has been done in two different ways. First, we have introduced time for the whole period (1980–81 to 2005–06), and then we have introduced an extra time dummy from 1991 onwards (1991–92 to 2005–06) in order to test the impact of economic reforms initiated in India in 1991. Let us now turn to Table 4.2, which presents the TFP changes for Indian ports. As evident from this table, except Kolkata port, rest 11 Indian ports come out with statistically significant TFP changes over the period from 1980–81 to 2005–06. In this table, TFP1 relates to the whole period and TFP2 relates to post-1991 period. These ports are: (i) Kandla with TFP value 0.062 (10.157), (ii) Mumbai with TFP value 0.032

Figure 4.3. Port-wise Y/L and K/L: 1980–81 to 2005–06

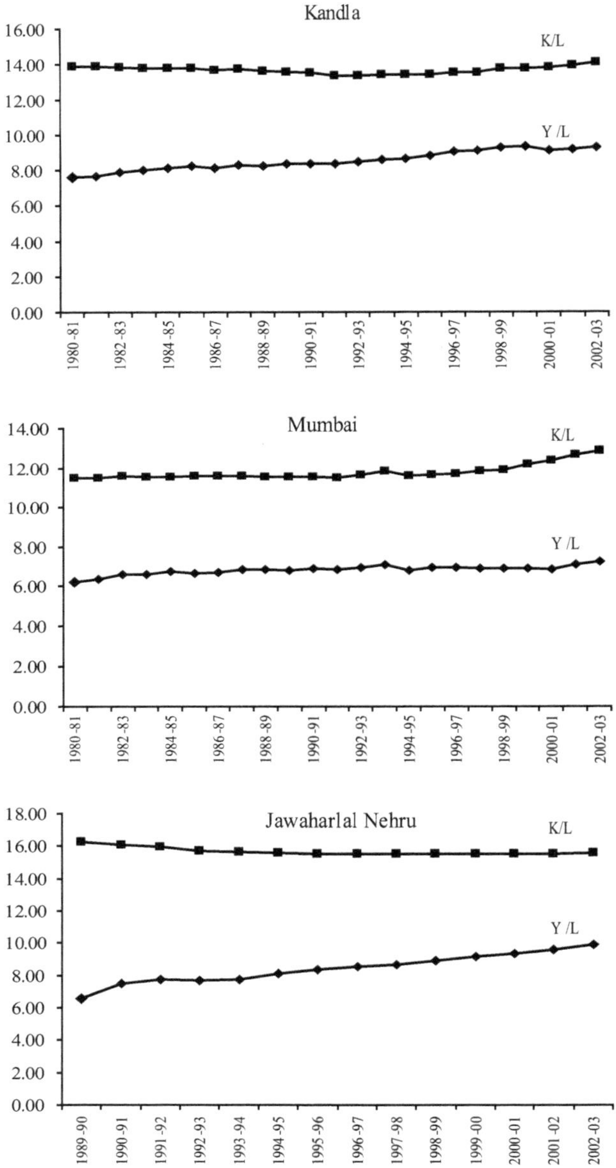

Figure 4.3. Port-wise Y/L and K/L: 1980–81 to 2005–06 (contd...)

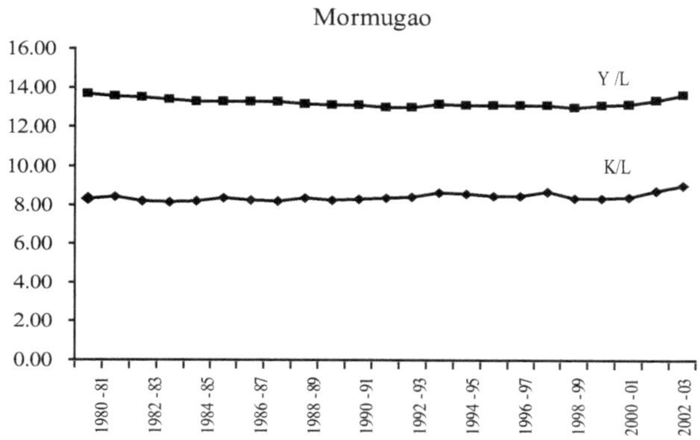

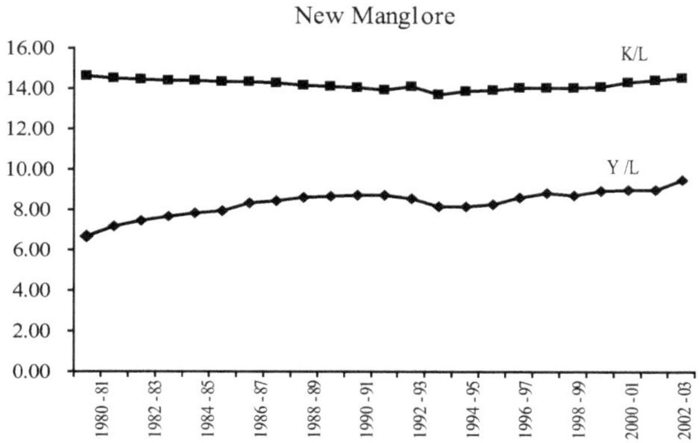

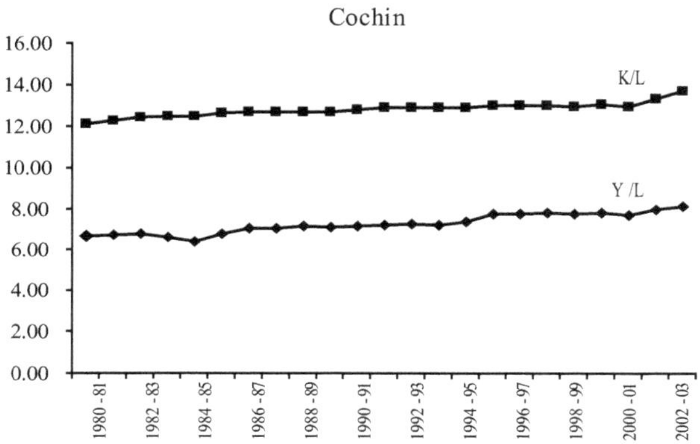

Figure 4.3. Port-wise Y/L and K/L: 1980–81 to 2005–06 (contd...)

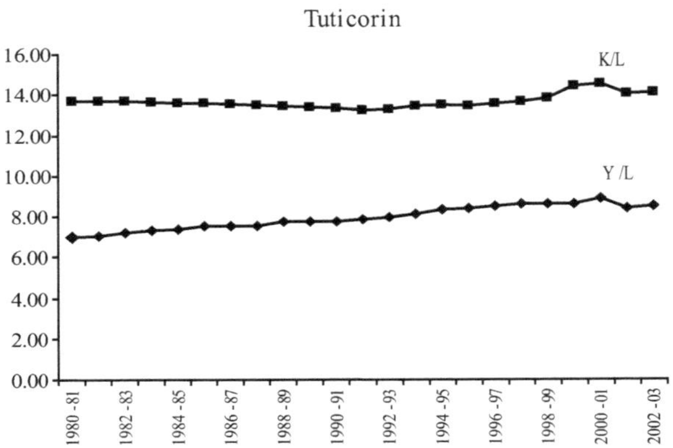

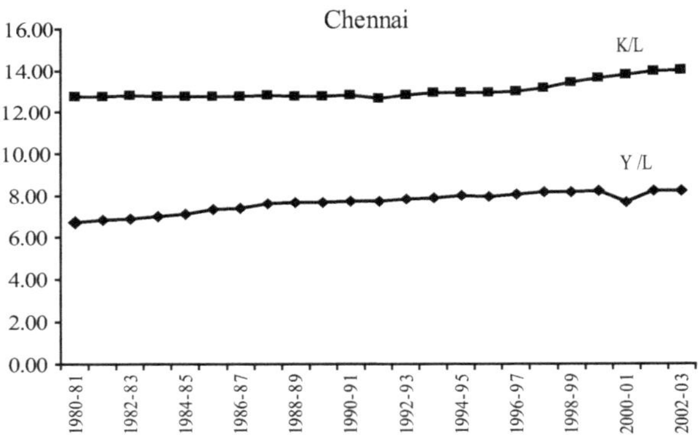

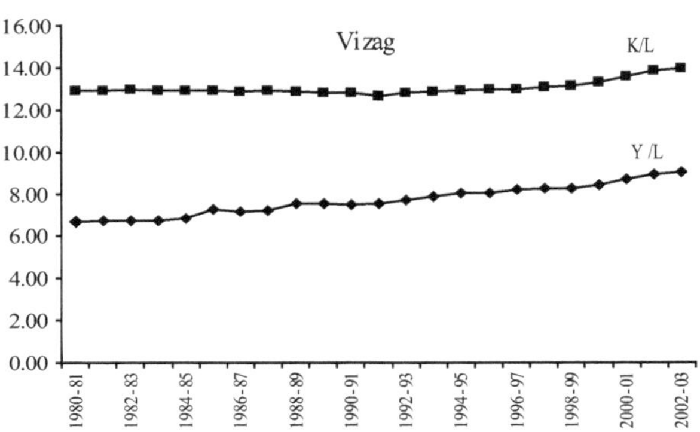

Figure 4.3. Port-wise Y/L and K/L: 1980–81 to 2005–06 (contd...)

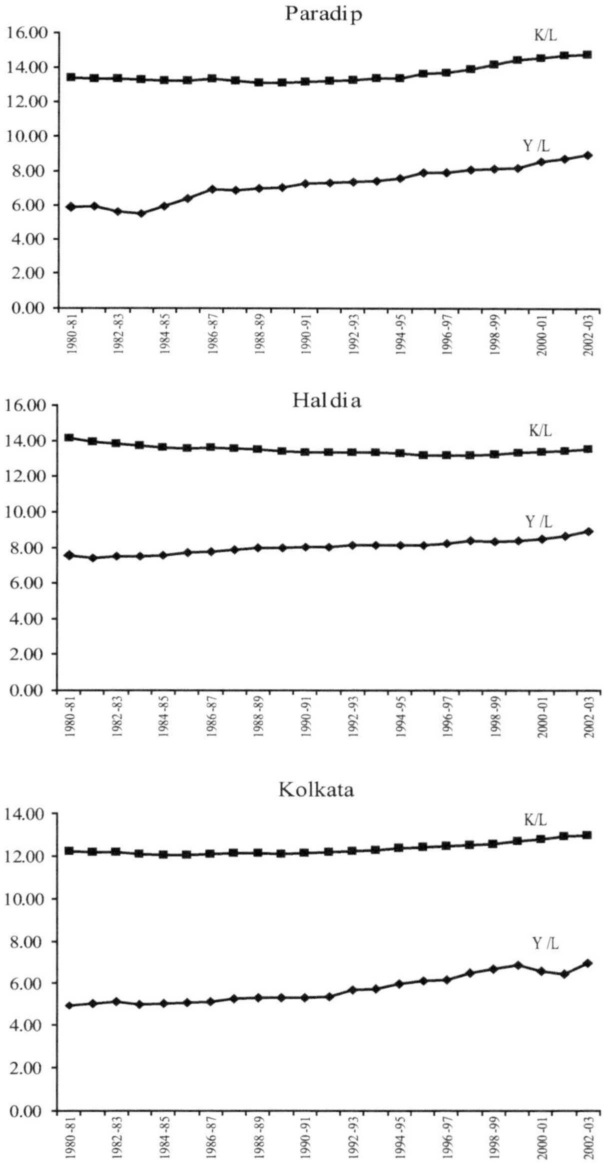

(6.922), (iii) Jawaharlal Nehru with TFP value 0.208 (8.840), (iv) Mormugao with TFP value 0.029 (11.901), (v) New Mangalore with TFP value 0.146 (11.74), (vi) Cochin with TFP value 0.067 (6.952), (vii) Tuticorin with TFP value 0.075 (31.662), (viii) Chennai with TFP value 0.103 (6.50), (ix) Vizag with TFP value 0.079 (8.225), (x) Paradip with TFP value 0.129 (6.652), (xi) Haldia with TFP value 0.085 (21.79), and Kolkata with TFP value –0.031 (–0.426) for the whole period from 1980–81 to 2005–06. The only port, which has registered negative TFP change, is Kolkata port.

Given the relative subjectivity of any statistical exercise concerning the valuation of capital, one should not stretch these results too far. Moreover, even if many studies relating to Indian ports consider 1980s at the loose beginning of the era of globalisation, we defer to draw any conclusion about these ports until we evaluate their performance in the post-reform period. Let us therefore turn to the same table with every second set of estimates corresponding to the same industries (TFP2). In this second set of output, TFP changes have been captured with a break from 1991–92 as the beginning of formal wide spread reforms. This may partially be taken to represent a general impact of reforms on the respective ports.

However, none of the ports has recorded statistically significant TFP change during the post-liberalisation period. However, only three ports have recorded positive TFP change during 1991–92 to 2005–06. These are: (i) Jawaharlal Nehru port with positive TFP value 0.178 (0.528), (ii) Mormugao port with positive TFP value 0.041 (0.611), (iii) and Kolkata port with positive TFP value 0.115 (0.803), but none is statistically significant. Interestingly, New Mangalore port has achieved statistically significant negative TFP change of –0.589 (–3.843) in the post-liberalisation period. Rest all ports have recorded negative TFP change for the same period. It is puzzling to observe that the earlier set of industries which has recorded significant TFP change from 1980–81 to 2005–06 have not come out to do anything significant during the post-reform period. This has both good and bad message for Indian economic reforms. The bad message is that economic environment in post-1991 period has not made any substantial impact on the performance of Indian ports in terms of TFP. The good message is that since our results have not found at least any substantial negative TFP growth (except New Mangalore) there are still many things to be done on the maritime front by the government. Or, in other words, the economic environment appears to have remained largely unchanged in terms of TFP performance during post-reform period.

A few words about the statistical properties of the TFP findings of these ports may be of interest here. First, introducing the time dummy since 1991 has strengthened the value of TFP change for the whole period. Second, except a few cases, the value adjusted R^2 and DW statistics show that the fitted results are not very erratic. Third, in most cases, labour has come out to be an important factor in this set up, whereas capital has not played any significantly positive role except for the port of Mormugao.

On the whole, as far as TFP change is concerned, most of the major ports have remained unchanged during the post-reform period except New Mangalore (with negative TFP change), which was found as one of the worst performing ports during the period 1985 to 2005 in previous chapters.

4.4 Summary and Conclusions

From the forgoing analysis, we have found that except Chennai, rest major ports of India, located on the east coast, have recorded higher growth rates in output (traffic) during the post-liberalisation period (1990–91 to 2005–06) than that of pre-liberalisation period (1980–81 to 1990–91). In case of major ports located on the west coast, except Cochin and Mormugao, growth rates of port traffic for rest major ports were decelerated in the post-liberalisation period. We have found mixed results in case of labour productivity. While, in the post-liberalisation period, Mumbai, New Mangalore, Tuticorin and Chennai have witnessed fall in labour productivities, rest of the major ports have witnessed rise in labour productivities during the same period. The steep rise of LP in Kolkata port in the post-liberalisation period is remarkable while the drastic fall of LP in case of New Mangalore port is a matter of serious concern. One of the interesting features of this growth analysis is that average annual growth rates of LP for most of the major ports have significantly outweighed those of traffic. Finally, except Haldia port, rest major ports have witnessed rise in K/L in the post-liberalisation period compared to that of pre-liberalisation period. This shows that the rise in K/L ratio is the result of a simultaneous increase in capital itself and decline in size of employment uniformly in all these ports except Haldia. This outcome in general indicates that Indian ports have been witnessing infusion of more capital as well as fall in employment in the post-liberalisation period, which, in other words, indicates Indian ports are becoming more capital intensive in the post-liberalisation period. The rise in K/L is the result of a widespread capital deepening process in Indian port sector.

With regard to TFP changes, except Kolkata port, rest 11 Indian ports came out with statistically significant TFP growth over the period from 1980–81 to 2005–06. The only port, which has registered negative productivity growth during the whole period, is Kolkata port. However, none of the Indian ports has recorded statistically significant positive TFP change during the post-liberalisation period. New Mangalore port is the only port which has achieved statistically significant negative TFP change in the post-liberalisation period. We have found that the earlier set of industries which has recorded significant TFP change from 1980–81 to 2005–06 have not come out to do anything significant during the post-reform period. This clearly indicates that economic climate in post-1991 period has not made any substantial impact on the performance of Indian ports in terms of the most popular measure of performance, TFP. It may further be concluded that the economic climate of the country appears to have remained largely unchanged in terms of TFP performance among Indian ports during the post-reform period.

There has been tremendous spurt in international research on the relationship between globalisation and productivity through either (i) a bias towards skilled worker, or (ii) application of higher technology, or both. If only the first factor is in operation, then there is a potential danger of rising unemployment and wage differential against the unskilled worker, which doubtless represent a larger share of the labour force in Indian port sector. If only the second factor is in operation, then ports having lower rate of capital accumulation (representing lower technological adaptation) will find it increasingly difficult to compete in a global market. Apart from the above, there may be differing impact on ports having inherently different labour-intensity and hence on the emerging nature of unemployment. Therefore, further study should be undertaken at much disaggregated level of classification.

Productivity of a port is the resultant of an economy's overall infrastructure networks including road, rail, electricity, housing, banking, postal and telecommunication facilities, demographic condition, irrigation facility, openness, labour policy, macro-economic stability (e.g. inflation rate) and the like. A long period causality test with aggregate productivity as well as public and private infrastructure capital for Indian ports are required for understanding the role of port in a comparable framework. As a corollary, an attempt should be made to identify the internal and external factors responsible for differential performance by Indian ports. As an extension of the findings of this chapter, we must also find what could be the impact of performance as a resultant of technological advancement on productivity in Indian ports. We will be dealing the latter proposal in the next chapters.

Productivity, Efficiency and Technological Change in Ports

5.1 Introduction

This chapter deals with the technological change in terms of its power and ability to improve the productivity of labour. Here, we try to study the effect of technological advancement as reflected in rising capital intensities on the productivity of labour in Indian ports.

Before the eighties of this century economists did not deal directly with factors such as transportation outfits, manufacturing belt and urbanisation, which explicitly exemplified the real existence of 'increasing returns'. Until recently, the relationship was rather asymmetric. For example, economic geographers abroad, while constructing their analytical theories and explanations of unbalanced regional development, have drawn heavily on the actual reality. But economists in less developed countries (LDCs) have tended to accord little if any attention to geographical factors in economic modelling even when they fail to find any economic justification for the same. The traditional logic that counters this argument points to the price mechanism that is supposed to take care of the forces of supply and demand. But it awfully fails to answer the problems of specialisation, trade orientation, increasing returns and hence regional inequality. So, issues of appropriate factor proportions for the transportation sector in the LDCs have not yet received due attention. Interestingly enough, economists in the developed countries have long been persuaded about the role of R&D in fostering technological advances in port sector in an era of globalisation which in turn help achieve faster productivity growth.[1]

A parallel literature in economic geography has been simultaneously trying to enrich the explanatory power of the regional development theory incorporating the impact of external sector on domestic economic development more specifically. Thus, over the past two decades a 'new trade theory' and a 'new economics of competitive advantage' have emerged which brought to the forefront the role that the internal geographical factors of an economy may play in determining the trading performance of that economy's industries as well as spread of economic activity.[2] Therefore, in order to understand the trading performance of a country we need to know the nature of supply of the trading instruments of the respective regions of the country from the points of production to the final outlet in the chain of transportation leading to the end point - port. This may be reflected in differing economic performance of various competing regions. Thus, the linkage from the production points to the shipment points through various intermediate transaction points in the chain of location is a very central theme of the process by which national economic prosperity and trade are created and maintained.

There is no denying the fact that the question of efficiency is inextricably related to the appropriateness of the chosen technology, and more often than not the fault may lie in the institutional preparedness for scientific management which is necessary for the smooth functioning of the new technology. Beyond the proximate source and from a broader technological perspective there may be certain features of the entire economic environment in a country that have a generally facilitating or retarding influence on growth (Rietveld and Nijkamp, 1993). In this context, productivity changes at the port level may be the resultant of the general efficiency at the macro level.

1 A non-conventional approach to the choice of technology by long periods of trial and error can be found in Ishikawa (1981). Moreover, numerous attempts have been made to measure the contributions of R&D to productivity growth, e.g., Griliches (1980), Nadiri (1980). Although they have used technological advance in a neoclassical context, the ultimate result is that the entire 'residual' part cannot be explained by spontaneous technological advance.

2 This new and popular wave of research works in the fields of 'new trade theory' and 'new economic geography' in a world of imperfect market was pioneered in a series of seminal works which started about two decades ago: Dixit and Stiglitz (1977), Johansson and Wigren (1996), Lancaster (1980), Krugman (1991, 1995), Porter (1990).

However, technological change in the port sector may be broadly defined to include (i) advances in technological knowledge embodied in new capital goods mostly imported from developed nations, which are affected by collaboration agreements undertaken between domestic and foreign firms, (ii) adaptive changes to be introduced by firms in the importing LDCs which are required to make the technology suitable for local conditions (including both process and product differentiations), and (iii) special tools and information about the techniques of scientific management.

We would like to deal with the first aspect of technological change in terms of its power and ability to improve the productivity of labour. Like any other LDC, India is characterised by acute scarcity of capital; awareness of how to make efficient use of existing resources through proper adjustment of policy variables is also sadly lacking. It is well known that if one of the two factors, capital and labour, increases at a very fast rate relative to the other, then the productivity of the other factor must increase at a faster rate. This chapter is concerned with the performance of Indian ports in terms of labour productivity (LP) in relation to capital coefficients. Or, in other words, we try to study the effect of technological advancement as reflected in rising capital intensities on the productivity of labour in Indian ports.

There are some studies, which have tried to understand the relationship between port performance and port traffic (Ghosh and De, 2000a; De and Ghosh, 2003), but none has touched upon the impact of technology on development of Indian ports under a liberal economic regime. Several reasons explain the choice of the Indian port sector. First, the port sector in several erstwhile developing countries has been undergoing transformation from a subsistence infrastructure resource into a more capital intensive, commercially and technologically oriented facility during last two decades (UNCTAD, 2001). On the other hand, India has been very late in taking the reform programme to her port sector. Indian ports are currently characterised by the existence of obsolete and poorly maintained equipment, hierarchical and bureaucratic management structures, weak coordination between the port trusts and users of the ports, lack of synchronisation of working times, excessive labour, and in general, an institutional framework that is considerably in variance with government's overall economic objectives. Second, considering the country's entry into the second stage of reform and when more than 75 percent of the country's foreign trade pass through seaports, the analysis will help to assess potential benefits of moving to a reformed port sector with advancement of better technology under a liberal trading regime.

This chapter proceeds as follows. Section 5.2 deals with the data and methodology. Section 5.3 outlines the concept and measurement of efficiency. Section 5.4 concentrates on the efficiency of input use in Indian ports in a comparative static framework over different time spans. In Section 5.5, an attempt is made to identify the factors influencing labour productivities in Indian ports. Finally, summary and policy implications are briefed in Section 5.6.

5.2 The Data

The period of this study falls between 1981–82 and 2005–06. The choice of the initial year (1981–82) is influenced by the fact that since the beginning of 1980s India for the first time was embarked upon a path of relative globalisation through liberal export import policy. A break at 1991–92 helps evaluate the impact of economic reforms on the port sector in the post-liberalisation period.

In general, port facility can be taken as public infrastructure input from the supply side. A period of 20 years is assumed to be adequate to check the extent of the impact of new technology on factor productivity. However, technological issues like adoption of indigenous technology, import of know-how and/or techniques are basically embodied in our analysis and not separately dealt with. To be specific, adoption of advanced capital-intensive techniques is proxied by increasing capital/labour ratios (K/L).

The major sources of data have been collected from various issues of (i) Basic Ports Statistics of India, (ii) Transport Statistics of India, and (iii) Profiles of Major Ports of India. Year-wise capital expenditures are converted into real terms with the help of gross domestic capital formation deflators (base 1993–94=100), collected from various issues of National Accounts Statistics, published by the Government of India. Port traffic (Y) and labour (L) are taken in physical quantities.

5.3 Concept and Measurement of Efficiency

Although methodological differences persist, there is a broad harmony in measuring productivity and efficiency of input use with the help of apparently different approaches. In existing literature, there are two different but interrelated techniques of measuring firm as well as industry efficiency. One is to proceed by estimating the average production function and the other by using the frontier production function (FPF), where the concept of 'best practice' method is used to locate the maximum potential output of firms using different input combinations at the prevailing state of technological knowledge.

In this study, a technique is said to be efficient (inefficient) when there is an upward (downward) shift of the productivity locus due to the adoption of new technology. Figure 5.1 graphically represents the concept of efficiency and in-efficiency respectively resulting from new technology adoption in a comparative static framework. In Figure 5.1(a), the curve LL is the labour-productivity locus prior to the adoption of new technology at time t_0. After adoption, the curve shifts to DD at time t_1 with corresponding higher values of Y/L. Let A be the observed position of a port on the old curve LL which shifts to C on DD after adoption. This movement from A to C can be divided into two parts. The first is from A to B which means that capital deepening process leads productivity to increase to B. But after adoption, productivity rises to C. The segment BC represents the gain in productivity due to efficient use of inputs with the help of advanced technology as manifested by higher capital per unit of labour (K/L).

Figure 5.1 Model for Measuring Efficiency

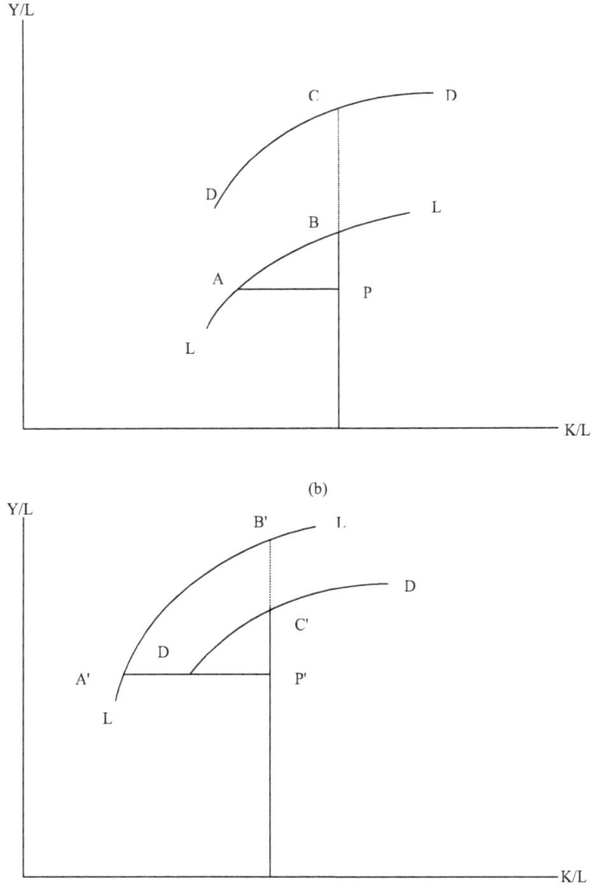

On the other hand, any downward shift of the locus is the consequence of inefficient use of inputs. The movement from A' to C' in Figure 5.1(b) is composed of two parts: A' to B' and B' to C'. Here as a reverse case of the drop in productivity from B' to C' is due to inefficient use of inputs even when productivity rises by P'C'. Thus, a rise in productivity does not necessarily mean efficient use of inputs when technology adoption augments the K/L ratio.

It may be mentioned here that port is an especial type of servicing unit. It is inextricably linked to a whole system of transportation network and the broader perspective of country's export-import policy, domestic consumption habitats and production base, availability of foreign exchange, geographical proximity to sea and natural breadth and depth of navigational channel. Given these natural and man-made externalities, performance of a port depends for all practical purposes upon how human behaviour render their all too important services for smooth functioning of the cargo management system. It is true that beyond a certain level, neither physical labour nor management authority has any perceptible control upon those natural external settings. But such argument is not unique against the empirical analysis of the port infrastructure. In fact, there is no production system in any 'economic society' which is independent of the 'geographical factors' a country is destined to. And in that sense, conventional tools of economic analysis is as suitable for the port sector as in any other. Therefore, in such a parametric approach, all types of internal and external influences upon the functioning of the cargo handling system are reduced to labour and capital.

5.3.1 The Model

This phenomenon of efficiency can be shown empirically from the relationship between observed LPs and K/L ratios across the ports for different points in time. The analysis is basically a macro relationship between LP and K/L. In this context, it may be mentioned that the linear homogeneous production function exhibiting constant returns to scale is equivalent to a function of one variable in per capita terms, i.e. LP = Y/L = f (K/L) where LP is output per labour. In our case, technological change in port infrastructure may be broadly understood to incorporate advances in the use of machinery and machine tools including construction as embodied in capital investment per unit of labour. To capture the inter-temporal shift, we have used temporal dummy variables. The empirical test for technological development employs multiple regressions of two non-linear equations of the forms:

$$\text{Ln (LP)} = \alpha + \beta_1 \text{ Ln (K/L)} + \beta_2 [\text{Ln (K/L)}]^2 + \beta_3 \text{D} \quad (5.1)$$

$$\text{Ln (LP)} = \alpha + \beta_1 \text{ Ln (K/L)} + \beta_2 [\text{Ln (K/L)}]^2 + \beta_3 \text{D} + \beta_4 [\text{Ln (K/L)}] \text{ D} \quad (5.2)$$

where D represents the temporal dummy with D=1 for latter years and D=0 for others, Y, K and L represent port traffic, capital and labour.

From equations 5.1 and 5.2 impact of K/L on LP over time can be estimated. Generally, the function dictates that in case of a positive association between the dependent and independent variables, the values of β_1, β_2 and β_3 should be greater than zero. However, the standard form of the production function specifically dictates here that the value of β_1 should be greater than zero while the value of β_2 should be negative. If the function shits upward (a special case where it moves in a northeastern direction), the value of β_3 will be positive. But if, $\beta_3 < 0$, this implies a downward shift of the productivity locus. Whether it shifts in a southeastern or southern direction, the production becomes inefficient in both the cases. Finally, β_4 represent the slope dummy of the curve. If $\beta_4 <0$, it implies that for large values of K/L the process becomes more inefficient. Positive values of β_3 and β_4 imply opposite results.

5.4 The Empirical Test of Efficiency

The empirical concept of technology is essentially an *ex post* economic characterisation where technological possibilities depend on various economic and institutional factors. An appropriate technology in one country may not be suitable for other where the economic and institutional settings differ. Since the development of a scenario of possible technologies with various combinations of economic characteristics is practically impossible, an appropriate technology developed with a view to using the factors efficiently may not produce the same result when applied to some other country (Ishikawa, 1981). In the LDCs, the usual practice is to import advanced technology from the developed nations but adaptation of this technology to local conditions requires continuous research involving huge time, expenditures and political willpower.[3]

The importance of innovation and rapidly changing technologies in the early and growth phases of the product cycle meant that the firms' own activities and many linked activities would need to be performed in more technologically-sophisticated regional settings. These areas were generally found to be (large) metropolitan places where the range of skilled engineers and other professionals, as well as appropriate subcontractors, was available. During the later phase of the product cycle, capital took on relatively more importance along with unskilled labour to bring unit costs into the line with those of imitating producers. Given that capital was relatively mobile, in some cases more so than labour, peripheral non-metropolitan regions and, increasingly, offshore locations became the principal places for branch operations (Scott, 1987).

Under this backdrop, we attempt to consolidate our findings in terms of the relationship between LP and K/L ratios in Indian major ports. Three scatter diagrams of the cross-section data on LP against K/L for three pair of years, 1981–82 and 2005–06, 1981–82 and 1990–91, and 1990–91 and 2005–06, have been presented in Figure 5.2. As evident from these diagrams, there exists some homogeneity among LPs for the lower values of K/L, while for the larger values a wide dispersion is observed. Another observation is that the points in all the three scatter diagrams show a tendency to move towards the northeastern direction over time. This shift indicates that (i) the major ports have become more capital using than before, and (ii) the productivities in general have

3 In the theoretical literature on growth, technological progress is conceived either as a 'free good' ('manna from heaven'), as a by-product (externality) of other economic activities, or as the result of international R&D activities in private firms. All three perspectives have some merits. Basic research in universities and other public R&D institutions provides substantial inputs to the innovation process. Learning by doing, using, interacting etc. are important for technological progress. However, it is now increasingly accepted, even among many neoclassical economists, that models that do not include the third source of technological progress (innovation as contributed by intentional activities in private firms) overlook one of the most important sources of technological progress in capitalist economies.

Figure 5.2. Scatter Diagram of Cross Section Data on Y/L against K/L

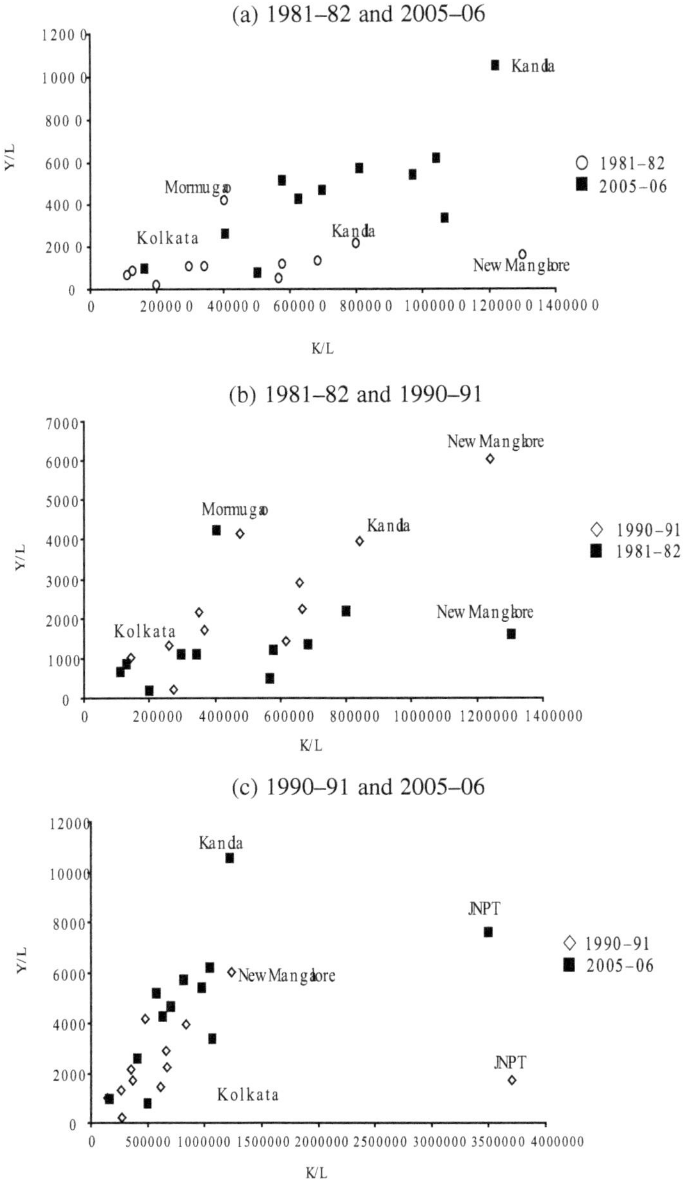

increased in the later year relative to K/L ratios. One prima facie observation is that Indian ports are fast becoming more and more capital-intensive with positive impact on productivities. Hence, the hypothesis of efficiency as raised earlier is supported by these scatter diagrams.

We have tried to unearth this phenomenon of efficiency in terms of shifts of the fitted curves (for equations 5.1 and 5.2) showing the relationship between LP and K/L for these combinations of years. As stated earlier, a functional relationship between Y/L and K/L is appropriate only when the production function is linear homogeneous. We have estimated the Cobb-Douglas production function for each of the three years twice, once imposing the homogeneity restriction of $\alpha + \beta = 1$, and once without this restriction. We have statistically tested the linear homogeneity property of the production function in our case using the data on all the 12 major ports. Appropriate F-tests based on the restricted and unrestricted error sum of squares have been performed. It is interesting to note from the correlation matrices given in the Table 5.1 that there does not appear to be any reversal of technological level across the ports over time. Moreover, the relationship between capital intensity and labour productivity is very consistent across the ports over time.

The estimated results of the OLS estimation of equations 5.1 and 5.2 are presented in the Table 5.2 with the values of the coefficients, t-statistics, adjusted R^2, Durbin-Watson statistic (serial correlation), standard error of estimates and F values for three combinations of data sets - (i) 1980–81 and 2005–06 (case-1), (ii) 1980–81 and 1990–91 (case-2) and (iii) 1990–91 and 2005–06 (case-3) separately. While case 1 explains the relationship between dependent and independent variables over an interval of 26 years, the later two cases evaluate the impact of pre- and post- liberalisation undertaken in July 1991. In case 1, Mormugao and Kolkata ports were omitted as outliers in equations 5.1 and 5.2 respectively. Jawaharlal Nehru port was not considered in cases 1 and 2 because the port was not in operation in 1980–81. In all the cases outlier detection was done on the basis of Cook's Distance Statistic. Hence, values of the parameters are estimated after omitting these ports. Interestingly, results vary over different pair of time spans thereby implying some sort of distinct nature of technological developments in

Table 5.1. Correlation Coefficients: Y/L and K/L

(a)

	Y/L(1)	K/L(1)	Y/L(2)	K/L(2)
Y/L(1)	1			
K/L(1)	0.257	1		
Y/L(2)	0.528	0.651	1	
K/L(2)	0.153	0.769	0.782	1

Notes:1. Y/L(1) & K/L(1) correspond to 1981–82.
2. Y/L(2) & K/L(2) correspond to 2005–06

(b)

	Y/L(1)	K/L(1)	Y/L(2)	K/L(2)
Y/L(1)	1			
K/L(1)	0.257	1		
Y/L(2)	0.672	0.844	1	
K/L(2)	0.281	0.993	0.842	1

Notes:1. Y/L(1) & K/L(1) correspond to 1981–82.
2. Y/L(2) & K/L(2) correspond to 1990–91

(c)

	Y/L(1)	K/L(1)	Y/L(2)	K/L(2)
Y/L(1)	1			
K/L(1)	0.131	1		
Y/L(2)	0.615	0.510	1	
K/L(2)	0.059	0.977	0.570	1

Notes:1. Y/L(1) & K/L(1) correspond to 1990–91.
2. Y/L(2) & K/L(2) correspond to 2005–06

Indian port sector. Among others, change of policy regimes might be responsible for such distinction over the last two decades. The overall percentage explained by the independent variables is much higher in case 1 for both equations. As evident from Table 5.2, overall result of case 2 (i.e., between the pair of years, 1980–81 and 1990–91) is too weak to judge any technological relationship among the variables over

Table 5.2. Regression Results

Observation year	Equation	Independent variables	Coefficient	t-values	Adj. R^2	SEE	DW	SC	F	N
1981–82 and 2005–06	1	Constant	58.528	1.389	0.682	0.57	1.77	0.091	14.55	20
		Log(K/L)	–8.753	–1.334						
		[Log(K/L)] Sq.	0.367	1.439						
		D	0.945	3.536						
	2	Constant	–24.089	–0.666	0.703	0.49	1.88	0.039	12.23	20
		Log(K/L)	4.589	0.809						
		[Log(K/L)] Sq.	–0.168	–0.755						
		D	–8.579	–1.828						
		Log(K/L) x D	0.722	2.036						
1981–82 and 1990–91	1	Constant	24.97	0.482	0.305	0.75	1.76	0.115	4.069	22
		Log(K/L)	–3.506	–0.433						
		[Log(K/L)] Sq.	0.163	0.519						
		D	0.486	1.524						
	2	Constant	14.884	0.281	0.304	0.75	1.56	0.211	3.291	22
		Log(K/L)	–1.738	–0.210						
		[Log(K/L)] Sq.	0.087	0.268						
		D	–5.878	–0.910						
		Log(K/L) x D	0.491	0.986						

Table 5.2 continued

Table 5.2 continued

Observation year	Equation	Independent variables	Coefficient	t-values	Adj. R^2	SEE	DW	SC	F	N
1990–91 and	1	Constant	–51.38	–1.876	0.464	0.65	1.76	0.116	7.64	24
2005–06		Log(K/L)	8.178	2.013						
		[Log(K/L)] Sq.	–0.281	–1.867						
		\D	0.468	1.713						
	2	Constant	–50.23	–1.828	0.462	0.65	1.58	0.202	5.931	24
		Log(K/L)	8.147	2.001						
		[Log(K/L)] Sq.	–0.285	–1.89						
		D	–4.064	–0.854						
		Log(K/L) x D	0.338	0.953						

Notes: 1. Dependent variable = Log(Y/L). 2. D = 0 for the first year, and = 1 for the second year in all cases.

this decade. As usual in a slow moving economy like India, relative liberalisation of 1984 failed to exert any technological repercussion on Indian ports as early as in 1990–91. On the other hand, the period between 1980–81 and 2005–06 witnesses significant technological improvements in terms of both equations.

Case 1 records statistically highly significant shift of the intercept dummy in the upward direction (positive). This bears clear testimony to a telling improvement in productivity through an upward shift of the

Figure 5.3. Fitted Relationship between Ln(Y/L) and Ln(K/L) with Temporal Dummy

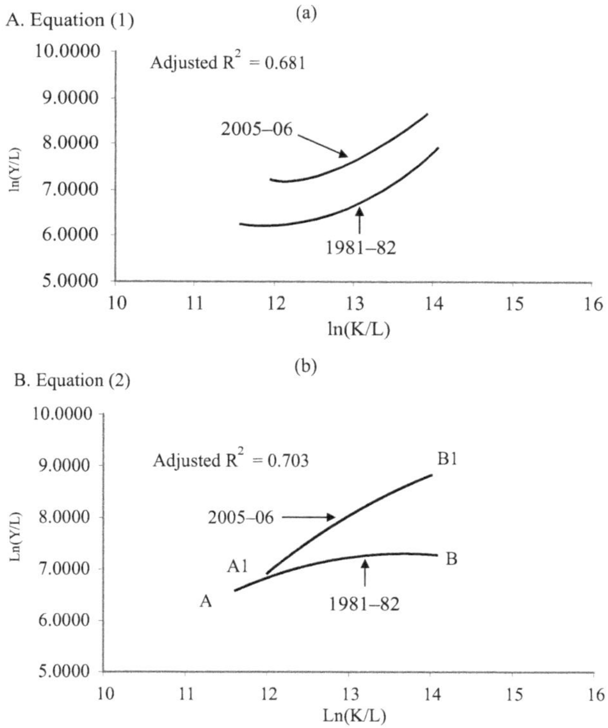

Note: Mormugao and Kolkata ports are deleted as outliers in Case (a) and Case (b) respectively and Jawaharlal Nehru port is omitted because it was not in operation in 1981–82.

productivity locus from AB to A_1B_1. In case 2, even if the intercept dummy is negative, a positive and significant slope dummy shifts the productivity locus for 2005–06 in the upward direction. The estimated results are drawn in Figure 5.3 (a, b). Statistically, inclusion of the slope dummy has reverted the direction of the productivity locus from one of exponential to downward sloping. This improvement over a period of 26 years may be the outcome of a natural rate of progression in a period of crucial importance for the Indian economy particularly from the viewpoints of foreign collaboration, technology import and open trade regime.

Figure 5.4. Fitted Relationship between Ln(Y/L) and Ln(K/L) with Temporal Dummy

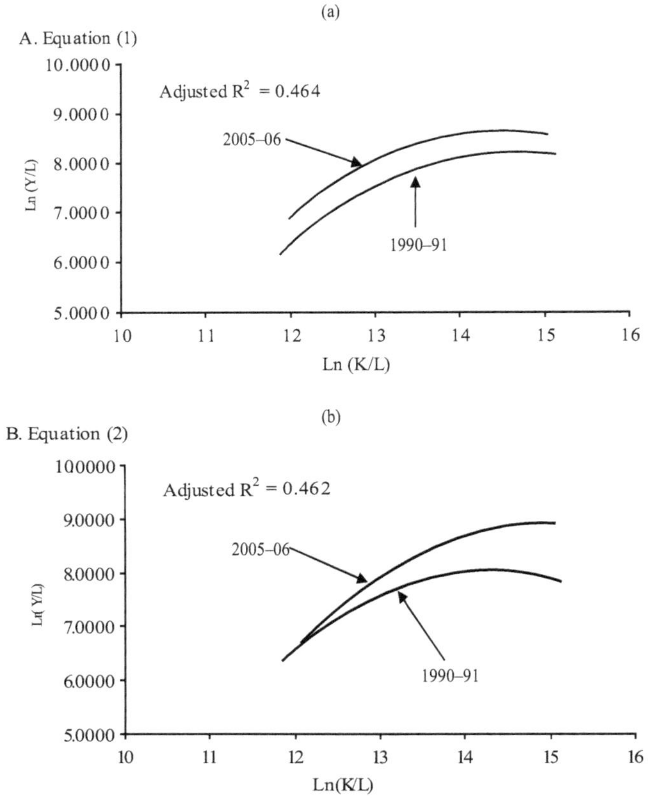

Our concern is more important with regard to the post-reform decade, that is, between 1990–91 and 2005–06. The estimated diagrams as presented in Figure 5.4 make it obvious that productivity increases with respect to capital intensity at a diminishing rate (for both equations). But inclusion of the slope dummy makes the time dummy statistically insignificant. Hence, better result is found with equation 5.1. That is, an upward shift of the productivity locus is observed between 1990–91 and 2005–06. Even if it is too early to proclaim as an impact of the open trade regime, it is noteworthy that Indian ports have recorded some sort of a technological improvement in the post-reform period.

5.5 Factors Influencing LP

Traditionally, efficiency in the port sector is influenced by both internal and external factors. To a large extent, the nature of influence of internal factors on productivity is linked with the intensity of inter- and intra-port competitions. Inter- and intra-port competitions depend on the level of development of the hinterland (the interior region served by each port) including good transport network. Attempts at explaining port competition in this fashion have also been extended to include other factors such as labour cost and productivity, rail connections, port access, and land availability (Kenyon, 1970; Mayer, 1978; Kuby and Reid, 1992; Hoyle, 1999). Normally, healthy competition among ports (or in between terminals of a port) helps improve overall efficiency of the port (Estache and de Rus, 2000).

Of particular interest, low efficiency in the Indian port sector as pointed out by De Monie (1995), Peters (1997), Haralambides and Behrens (2000), and Ghosh and De (2000b) may be due to a number of factors, both internal and external, such as (i) management quality, (ii) skill, (iii) financial positioning, (iv) operational performance like turnaround time, utilisation of berths and equipments, (v) external factors like reliability and quality of input supply, (vi) logistics network,

(vii) degree of internal competition, (viii) navigational factors like draft of the river/sea, (ix) industrial agglomeration, and (x) overall health of the economy. But in view of the fact that efficiency here is defined in terms of intertemporal productivity changes, we have chosen a set of supply-side factors which are likely to influence the level of and changes in productivity.

We have tried two types of regressions (linear and log-linear) with various combinations of the explanatory variables in order to identify the factors which determine LP in the aggregate. The dependent variable is LP – real value added per employee. The independent variables are (i) K/L, (ii) SKILL – measured by the ratio of skilled personnel (all employees minus daily wageworkers) to all employees, (iii) TRT – ship Turn-Round Time, which is the duration of the vessel's stay in port and is calculated from the time of arrival to the time of departure, (iv) RRT - Rate of Return on Turnover, derived from operating surplus divided by operating income of a port. We performed these regressions only for two combinations of data sets - (i) 1990–91 and 2005–06 (case 1), and (ii) 1981–82 and 2005–06 (case-2) separately. While Case 2 identifies factors which influence LP in the overall period, Case 1 helps to know the same in the post-liberalisation period. Both linear and log-linear results of all the regressions are presented in Table 5.3.

For the first set of equations (linear forms), the most important variable (judged by the level of significance) in the determination of LP is K/L as before. This candidly indicates that capital alone determines the labour productivity in the Indian port sector in both pre- and post-liberalisation periods. Significance level of K/L also gets stronger in the post-liberalisation period. Why K/L alone decides the fate of LP? One plausible reason may be that large amount of capital expenditure was incurred for (a) modernisation of berths and cargo handling equipments, (b) specialised services and (c) container handling facilities as a result of on-going worldwide reorientation of the port sector. A look at Table 5.4 makes it clear about the growing use of modern container handling equipments in the Indian port sector in the post-liberalisation period.

However, dropping the K/L, we find RRT as the second most influential factor in determining LP. As reported in all different combina-

Table 5.3. Estimated Coefficients of Regression on LP

Equation form: Linear   Dependent variable = LP

(a)

Observation years	Independent variables	Coefficient	t-values	Adj. R^2	SEE	F	DW	SC	N
Case 1.1990–91	Intercept	–955.77	–0.30	0.58	1578	8.24	2.00	–0.02	22
and 2005–06	K/L	0.01	3.31			(4, 17)			
	SKILL	4.93	0.14						
	RRT	23.62	0.56						
	TRT	–25.05	–0.15						
	Intercept	475.21	0.12	0.35	1968	4.71	2.18	–0.11	22
	SKILL	4.67	0.11			(3, 18)			
	RRT	123.52	3.31						
	TRT	–248.59	–1.31						
	Intercept	–985.31	–0.38	0.62	1506	17.93	1.95	0.01	22
	K/L	0.01	5.79			(2, 19)			
	SKILL	8.30	0.26						
Case 2.1980–81	Intercept	474.18	0.1	0.42	1970	4.75	1.7	0.05	20
and 2005–06	K/L	0.003	2.59			(4, 17)			
	SKILL	9.37	0.17						
	RRT	53.35	1.64						
	TRT	–211.6	–1.28						
	Intercept	1190.3	0.54	0.45	1916	6.69	1.67	0.06	20
	K/L	0.004	2.72			(3, 18)			
	RRT	54.46	1.76						
	TRT	–210.28	–1.3						

Equation form: Log-Linear Dependent variable = LP

(b)

Observation years	Independent variables	Coefficient	t-values	Adj. R^2	SEE	F	DW	SC	N
Case 1.1990–91	Intercept	–3.07	–0.54	0.58	0.58	8.21	1.52	0.23	22
and 2005–06	Log(K/L)	0.72	2.60			(4, 17)			
	Log(SKILL)	0.02	0.02						
	Log(RRT)	0.73	1.63						
	Log(TRT)	–0.66	–1.60						
	Intercept	6.45	1.29	0.44	0.66	6.59	1.89	0.02	22
	Log(SKILL)	–0.36	–0.32			(3, 18)			
	Log(RRT)	1.43	3.49						
	Log(TRT)	–1.09	–2.51						
	Intercept	–9.32	–1.85	0.53	0.61	12.78	1.46	0.27	22
	Log(K/L)	1.09	4.95			(2, 19)			
	Log(SKILL)	0.63	0.64						
Case 2.1980–81	Intercept	–1.81	–0.25	0.53	0.68	6.99	1.00	0.48	20
and 2005–06	Log(K/L)	0.64	2.78			(4, 17)			
	Log(SKILL)	0.88	0.59						
	Log(RRT)	0.36	1.26						
	Log(TRT)	–1.80	–2.59						
	Intercept	1.86	0.51	0.55	0.70	9.55	0.94	0.51	20
	Log(K/L)	0.65	2.89			(3, 18)			
	Log(RRT)	0.38	1.36						
	Log(TRT)	–1.80	–2.64						

Notes: 1. Jawaharlal Nehru Port was omitted in both cases. While this port was found as outlier following Cook's Distance Statistic in Case 1, it was not considered in Case 2 as the port was not in operation in 1980–81. 2. Figures in parentheses represent degree of freedom.

tions of regressions, there appears to be a strong relationship between capital intensity and rate of return. This is logically very consistent because higher rate of return and higher capital intensity work in the same direction. That is, technological level facilitates the opportunities for better rate of return thereby indicating the presence of scale economies. As a matter of fact, we have observed higher RRT in the Indian port sector in the post-1991 period (see Table 5.5).

Interestingly, contrary to popular belief, SKILL does not significantly influence LP in this analysis. Perhaps, when all the major ports run with more or less a sort of outdated technology and large pool of unutilised labour forces (over-manning), Indian ports are yet to find importance of skilled and specialised manpower. For example, when the port of Singapore clears a container vessel in a couple of hours, any Indian port takes 3 to 4 days by applying mixed pool of skilled and unskilled labour forces and semi-advanced technology under a scarce financial health of the port. This means skilled manpower still has very limited impact on overall labour productivity of the port.[4]

As expected, TRT has always produced negative sign in all the regressions, although in most cases it is not statistically important. This may perhaps be due to the fact that on an average most of the Indian

4 Current arrangements for cargo handling at some Indian ports in the container segment are not conducive for fast handling and turnaround. These ports namely Mumbai, Cochin, Kolkata and Haldia rely on ship's own gear instead of any modern shore-side gantry cranes. Due to this, move of boxes per hour is abysmally low and thereby a port takes 3 to 4 days to clear a vessel from the berth. These shortcomings are especially critical for the container trade, as the waiting cost of capital-intensive container vessels is high. In the break bulk sector, the situation is much more dire. Mumbai port being one of the busiest ports of the country normally unloads 2000 tonnes of per day and takes nearly 15 days to unload 20,000 tonnes of break bulk cargo (Mody, 2001). The amazing disparity in the level of technology (and hence the demand for skilled labourers) between Indian and other advanced Asian ports may be understood from the following example: When India's all major ports together handle about 2.5 million container boxes per annum by deploying only 20 rail mounted gantry cranes (RMGC) and 40 rubber tyred gantry cranes (RTGC), Laem Chabang port (in Thailand) alone handles more than 2 million TEUs by deploying 24 RMGCs and 50 RTGCs.

Table 5.4. Container Handling Facilities at Indian Ports

Port#	Container Traffic ('000 TEUs)		No of Berths		No of SGCs*		No of RTGs**	
	1990–91	2005–06	1990–91	2005–06	1990–91	2005–06	1990–91	2005–06
Jawaharlal Nehru	88	2667	2	6	2	16	4	49
Mumbai	230	156	6	4	2	2	2	3
Cochin	20	203	1	2	0	2	1	4
Tuticorin	15	321	0	1	0	2	0	4
Chennai	67	735	1	3	1	4	2	10
Vizag	0	47	0	1	0	2	0	4
Haldia	8	110	1	2	0	0	1	1
Kolkata	60	203	4	4	0	0	1	3

Notes: * Shore-side Gantry Cranes in the range between 35 tonnes to 40 tonnes. ** Rubber Tyred Gantry Cranes in the range between 35 tonnes to 40 tonnes. # Combined share in Indian total container traffic is more than 85% in 2005–06.
Source: Indian Ports Association, New Delhi

Table 5.5. Rate of Return on Turnover (RRT) in Indian Ports

(%)

Ports	1985–86		1991–92		1999–2000		2005–06	
	SIPT*	RRT	SIPT*	RRT	SIPT*	RRT	SIPT*	RRT
Kandla	11.22	48.28	13.00	33.54	16.40	50.43	10.84	31.99
Mumbai	18.65	34.91	19.02	31.06	12.20	36.81	10.44	30.27
Jawaharlal Nehru	–	–	1.34	16.60	6.20	43.18	8.91	59.67
Mormugao	16.88	36.98	9.80	11.45	6.10	24.16	7.48	35.63
New Mangalore	2.04	20.78	5.28	42.16	5.00	50.99	8.14	52.85
Cochin	5.88	11.06	4.80	18.76	5.25	31.34	3.29	32.12
Tuticorin	3.20	39.84	3.34	32.46	4.00	46.91	4.05	61.29
Chennai	13.04	44.38	16.14	44.01	14.50	39.86	11.16	27.51
Ennore	–	–	–	–	–	–	2.17	57.20
Vizag	13.10	33.36	12.78	24.54	14.00	38.54	13.18	54.00
Paradip	3.02	1.14	4.50	32.97	5.00	39.09	7.82	48.98
Kolkata	5.85	–3.13	2.70	9.30	4.00	39.46	2.55	31.64
Haldia	7.12	30.13	7.30	32.81	7.35	39.46	9.97	25.37
Average		27.07		27.47		40.02		42.19

Notes: * Share in Total Indian Port Traffic. – Not in operation.

Source: Various issues of Basic Port Statistics of India, Ministry of Shipping, Road Transport and Highways, Government of India

ports are yet to achieve a swift turnaround of vessels, which is still is hovering around 4 to 5 days (see Table 5.6). There is a group of services related to turnaround of vessels, which include pilotage, towing and tying, berthing, loading and unloading, and ancillary activities. In general, Indian port authorities are still solely responsible for all such services, which are associated with vessel's turnaround. Being an important catalyst for overall improvement of productivity, these services need immediate reform. Here, government may think for different operators, public and/or private, for different services instead of one authority for many services.

An almost similar set of results is obtained when we consider the second set of equations (log-linear forms). The values of the adjusted R^2 have improved in all the equations compared to their linear counterparts. However, combining both the results it is evident that K/L has played the most vital role in determining LP.

Table 5.6. Average Turnaround Time of Indian Ports

(Days)

Ports	1991–92	1995–96	1999–2000	2005–06
Kandla	12.53	9.43	7.56	4.39
Mumbai	10.44	8.44	6.04	4.06
Jawaharlal Nehru	5.66	4.67	2.94	1.97
Mormugao	8.49	5.39	4.84	6.06
New Mangalore	6.50	4.35	3.75	3.00
Cochin	6.90	4.06	3.61	2.70
Tuticorin	7.56	5.22	4.23	2.83
Chennai	9.44	6.2	6.58	3.32
Ennore	–	–	–	2.23
Vizag	8.34	6.06	5.01	3.79
Paradip	8.28	7.55	4.16	3.56
Kolkata	10.23	8.37	6.25	4.12
Haldia	8.44	7.36	4.14	4.89
All Ports (Average)	8.57	6.43	4.93	3.63

Source: Various issues of Basic Port Statistics of India, Ministry of Shipping, Road Transport, and Highways, Government of India

5.6 Summary and Implications

This study examined (i) the impact of advanced technology which is proxied by rising K/L ratios in Indian port sector on the efficiency of factor use, and (ii) the factors influencing labour productivities across major ports. First, increasing use of overhead capital has produced significant improvement in productivities. Second, there is ample evidence in favour of upward shift of the productivity locus. In essence, this implies that the major ports of India have witnessed some kind of technological metamorphosis between 1980–81 and 2005–06. Third, the most important factors that influence labour productivities in an aggregate sense are the capital/labour ratio, and rate of return on turnover; interestingly, ship turnaround time and port's skilled human resources do not play any significant role in determining labour productivity.

These findings have important implications for technology policy in the port sector in LDCs and particularly in India. Before India began reforming its port system in 1990s, her ports were costly and inefficient. As a result of all these problems, Indian ports were loosing market share to the more efficient Sri Lankan and Singaporean ports and also to the road sector. Rising inefficiencies in ports have forced the governments to deregulate the port system with the objective of increasing financial viability, productive efficiency and transfer of appropriate technology.[5]

5. India's port reforms literally began in 1997 when a newly elected Government, facing an exceptionally severe criticism from the developed world for not having a modern port, embarked on privatisation of Jawaharlal Nehru Port with a longer-term programme of comprehensive structural reforms in the existing major (government) ports. The basic purpose of port reform is to encourage specialisation of services which was recognized long back by both the classical economists like Adam Smith, and the pioneers of development economics like Myrdal and Hirschman. Adam Smith's emphasis on geography goes through the transport mechanism which strengthens his classic sequence of division of labour followed by productivity and specialisation with market expansion in a free trade regime.

To reduce costs and increase productivity, the Indian reform strategy sought to deregulate, decentralise, and organise inter- and intra-port competitions. As performance indicators for Jawaharlal Nehru port show, the improvements have been dramatic since the privatisation of the port in 1997. Port charges and shipping tariffs have declined sharply, and labour and berth productivities have improved in Jawaharlal Nehru port. Since improved performance leads to higher traffic[6], it now witnesses higher traffic. In 1997, Jawaharlal Nehru port used to handle only 500,000 TEUs, and now it hits the target of 4 million TEUs and became India's major container port. By privatising its container berth to international terminal operators like DP World, Maersk, its' overall terminal productivities have improved substantially. Now, world's renowned liners are offering regular Panamax vessel services at Jawaharlal Nehru port thereby indicating growing interest of liners. Due to this, users are sending their goods at a lower rate and delivering it at much reduced time through more direct calls of Panamax vessels. This achievement is pretty staggering preciously because this facility is absolutely new in this port and yet to be completed even. Having seen the success of reform, Indian government therefore, has started leasing out container berths of other major ports through competitive bidding.

The level of technological development in Indian ports is such that they even did not use modern container handling equipments even a decade ago. Now, due to the reforms, ports are trying to install sophisticated modern equipments at its terminals run by private operators which have created opportunities for skilled and specialised personnel. This has resulted in phenomenal increase in productivity. If we look at the

6 While it is true that lack of overseas traffic makes the port idle, some studies have shown that port has to keep improving its performance level to work ahead in the area of competition and most of the Indian ports provide evidence towards the fact that performance causes traffic (Ghosh and De, 2001). Poor port performance also results in weak nodes in the international transport network. The President of Russian Federation quoted losses of $ 1.5 billion per year due to poor port services and noted that 70 million tonnes of national cargo are now being transited via Finnish and Baltic ports (UNCTAD, 2001).

performance of terminal operators separately from that of respective port authority, we will find encouraging results. Now, some of the container terminals managed by some port holding companies like PSA at Tuticorin (India), DP World at Jawaharlal Nehru, Chennai, Cochin, Vizag (India), Evergreen at Laem Chabang (Thailand), and Hutchinson at Port Klang (Malaysia) and Shanghai (China) are handling container boxes with more or less at the same pace; one shore side quay crane of all these four terminals now moves average 25 TEUs per hour. This integration of cargo handling activities has led to encourage necessity for adequate skilled personnel in the port sector.

In this short time span two broad lessons have emerged from India's port reform, which have changed the way Indian port authorities used to function a decade ago. Firstly, competition can be effective – both among and within ports. Secondly, commitment of the government is vital in regulating the game even after port services have been privatised. While some dramatic results have been obtained from the first lesson, more path breaking actions are required in the second category to give a full shape of the deregulation process.[7] Here, fundamental restructuring and changes in management culture within the Indian port system are to be initiated through gradual labour management coordination. When the objective of port reform in general is to improve performance and efficiency by distancing government from day to day operations,

7 The privatisation strategy adopted by the Indian government worked well in case of Jawaharlal Nehru port, but it is yet to generate desired results in case of Tuticorin port where 370 meters quay line was leased to the PSA Corporation in 1999 to run a modern container terminal. Although this terminal is having 14 meters navigable and berthing draft, and also is highly equipped with modern cargo handling equipments (4 RMGCs and 4 RTGs), and is, it handles 1/4th of what P&O Ports handles at Jawaharlal Nehru port. So question often arises about the degree of inter-port competition. There is no universal rule for the degree of competition and regulation desirable in a port with a particular volume of traffic, but for container ports there is acceptance of some thresholds (Kent and Hochstein, 1998; Estache and de Rus, 2000). Perhaps, in India, low container market size decides the intensity of inter-port competition and thereby the fate of newly built private container terminals.

which was seen to be the cause of poor port performance, the government, as regulator, still has immense role to play because even though reform has improved port performance (Hirst, 2000; De and Ghosh, 2003) but dissatisfaction persists with the various reform models which have failed to establish competition. Clearly the objective has not been met and naturally political input continues to impede commercial objectives. A few giant ports, arising due to improved performance, are fast entering to each others' market with or without collusive arrangements which is working against the competitive nature of the market and the globalisation process (Trujillo and Serebrisky, 2003; De and Park, 2003, 2004). Naturally, anti-competitive behaviour of terminal operators has already become an important issue in the post-reform period. Hence, government has to ensure a competitive market by removing the inequality among the ports without which ports may not be able to sustain their performance in long run. The next chapter discusses this particular aspect of market concentration in context of Indian port sector.

Concentration and Competition in Ports

6.1 Introduction

The focus of this chapter is to measure the concentration and competition in Indian port sector. Intra-port competition is widely regarded as beneficial, for the competitiveness of ports, for local and national economies, and for consumers and exporting industries.

In an open economy, growth of large ports may contribute to the concentration that arises – in general, through the accumulation of other port's hinterlands or through internal growth. According to Tschoegl (1982), concentration is a social issue because it is conducive to cartelistic and oligopolistic behaviour and it alters the power of the economic structure. In the presence of high concentration, a relatively small group of ports run simultaneously across the system, employing similar methods and conventions of analysis and behaviour. Such a practice may help to determine, in part, the port tariff and service manipulation among key ports in the system. Furthermore, during economic downturns and a fall in trade, a decline in traffic and deterioration of a capital position of some ports in the system may develop into a major port sector crisis. The larger the port concentration, the larger is the potential severity of losing out in international trade.

A port grows by virtue of the trade it attracts. Inefficient ports, whether through lack of an integrated transport network, outdated work practices, or obsolete facilities, can stall a country's export-led growth, and also generate anti-competitive forces. Restrictive labour regulations, coupled with inefficient operating practices, spread the inequality of the port system. A fall in inequality among ports can mean the rapid rise in the value of commodities handled, or a shift from lower grade to higher grade goods, particularly among exports, or an absolute diversion of traffic away from the larger ports to smaller and better equipped ports (Kuby and Reid,

1992). Despite the considerable fluctuation of international trade by ports year to year in India, one sees a picture of general growth of container traffic among the ports located along India's west coast.

Some several years have passed since India embarked on port reforms. Since that time some important ports – Jawaharlal Nehru, Tuticorin, Chennai, Vizag, Haldia – were partly privatised. With the exception of Kolkata and Mumbai ports which opted for slow commercialisation, all other major ports in the country have set in place some form of reformed model. The objective of port reform in general in most of the countries is to improve performance and efficiency by distancing government from day to day operations which has been seen to be the cause of poor port performance. Undoubtedly reform has improved performance of port (Hirst, 2000; De and Ghosh, 2002), but dissatisfaction persists that the various reform models have failed to establish competition in the industry. Clearly the objective has not been met and naturally political input continues to impede commercial objectives. A few giant ports are fast entering to each others' market with or without collusive arrangements, which is working against the competitive nature of the market and the globalisation process (De, 1999; Trujillo and Serebrisky, 2003; De and Park 2003, 2004).

While commentators (Hirst 2000; Everett, 2002) argue that political interference is the cause of port inefficiency this is a somewhat erroneous and myopic view. After initiating reform process of a decade or so when we find port system is working against competitive forces, it is very difficult to say whether political interference is the cause of port inefficiency or it is an effect of something more endemic of a model and legislative framework which is encouraging anti-market competitive forces. The more container traffic is concentrated in the hands of a few ports, the more inequality there is; and the larger the shares of the largest terminal operator in the container ports, the more concentration there is in this port. Rise in concentration over a long period of time generate anti-competitive forces between ports and within ports (Tschoegl, 1982).

In our particular case, antitrust behaviour of terminal operators has already become an important issue. Liner companies have become larger as a result of mergers and acquisitions and global terminal operators

Table 6.1 Global Terminal Operators' Share of World Container Traffic

(%)

Terminal Operators	2005	2006	2007
HPH	13	13	14
PSA	11	12	11
APM	10	10	12
DPI*	9	10	9
COSCO Pacific	7	7	8
Eurogate	3	3	3
SSA Marine	3	3	3
Total	56	58	60
World container traffic (million TEUs)	387.7	434.3	485.0

Note: *DP International includes CSX World Terminals and P&O Ports for all three years.
Source: UNCTAD (2008)

have emerged because of investment opportunities driven by port privatisation.[1] Today, the world's top ten carriers have nearly 50 percent of the world's container carrying capacity, while the world's top seven terminal operators, including HPH, PSA, APM, DPI, COSCO Pacific, Eurogate, SSA Marine handle about 60 percent of world's port container volume (Table 6.1). The emerging dominance of these firms, at least in the port industry, has not gone unnoticed as their antitrust behaviour is being debated and challenged (Kent, 2002; De and Park, 2004; Yap et al, 2006). In case of India, DPI (Dubai Ports International) with its five container terminals (in Jawaharlal Nehru, Cochin, Chennai, Mundra and Vizag ports) share about 60 percent of country's annual container traffic. The rising dominance of DPI in India, however, has gone relatively unnoticed. There are some studies (Kent and Ashar, 2001; Kent, 2002), which have dealt antitrust behaviour of international terminal operators, but, none so far has touched upon the same in case of Indian private terminals operators. The contrast is while there has been an upward change in productivity and efficiency in Indian ports over time, public sector monopoly is being apparently replaced by the pri-

1 For a good discussion of concentration trends, see Hoffman (1998, 2002).

vate sector, whereas one of the major objectives of port privatisation has been to encourage competition. Given above, our objective in the present chapter is to investigate formal properties of rising concentration of the Indian port system and the evolving competition structure.

The organisation of the chapter is as follows. Section 6.2 deals with the data and methodology. Inequality among Indian ports and ports of maritime states are discussed in section 6.3. Section 6.4 deals with the relationship between port performance, cargo composition and hinterland's output. Section 6.5 elaborates on the degree of openness, port traffic and port capacity. Section 6.6 presents trends in concentration and competition in port industry. Section 6.7 deals with policy issues. Finally, summary, implications and future research agenda are briefed in Section 6.8.

6.2 Data and Methodology

For the present purpose, we have organised the following data for nine Indian coastal states over the period from 1970 to 2005. Net State Domestic Product (NSDP), as given by the Central Statistical Organisation (CSO), are defined as the net value added (after depreciation is accounted for) originating in each states, representing here as output. Here, we have gone a step further from the prevalent practices for the conversion of nominal NSDP into real term. Following Ghosh, Marjit and Neogi (1998), we have used Consumer Price Indices for Agricultural Labourers (CPIAL) with base, 1960–61=100 for deflating nominal Per Capita Net State Domestic Product (PCNSDP).[2]

2 The series of available CPIAL are large enough for the period of present study. But it is not available for all the States. Hence for those States for which the Government does not estimate it we have proxied by the CPIAL of the most adjacent and comparable State. This replacement is even preferable to WPI and CPI for industrial workers of the all-India type.

Another major data used for this chapter relate to port and related facilities. In Indian context, port related services can be understood as public infrastructure input from the supply side. As shown in Chapter 2, we have taken eight important variables for major ports of India for four different time points over the period from 1985 to 2005 to judge their relative performance.

The data for the analysis in this chapter are collected from the following sources: (i) Estimates of State Domestic Products, (ii) Economic Survey, (iii) Statistical Abstract, (iv) National Accounts Statistics, (v) Basic Ports Statistics of India and (vi) Transport Statistics of India - all published by the Government of India. This data set is supplemented by various publications of (i) the Centre for Monitoring Indian Economy (CMIE), Mumbai, (ii) India Database - The Economy by H. L. Chandok and The Policy Group, (iii) India Infrastructure Database 2005 (Ghosh and De, 2005), and various publications of Indian Ports Association (IPA), New Delhi.

6.3 Inter-port Comparison of Traffic over Time

Traditionally, the study of competition among ports has focused on the hinterlands (this is the interior region served by each port), and initially defined on the basis of the rail rates from the ports to the interior (Mayer, 1978). Later, port competition studies began to consider forelands (the overseas region served by each port) and the combined water-port-land rate advantages (Weigend, 1958; Draine, 1963). Continuing with this development, explanations of port competition have been extended to include other factors such as labour costs and productivity; rail connections; port access; and land availability (Kenyon, 1970; Mayer, 1978). Hoare (1986) found overlapping hinterlands of UK ports, and concluded that the concept of relatively exclusive port hinterlands no longer applies as well as it once did. Hinterland has been defined as 'organised and developed land space which is connected with a port by means of transport

Figure 6.1. Lorenz Curve for Port System of Major Ports

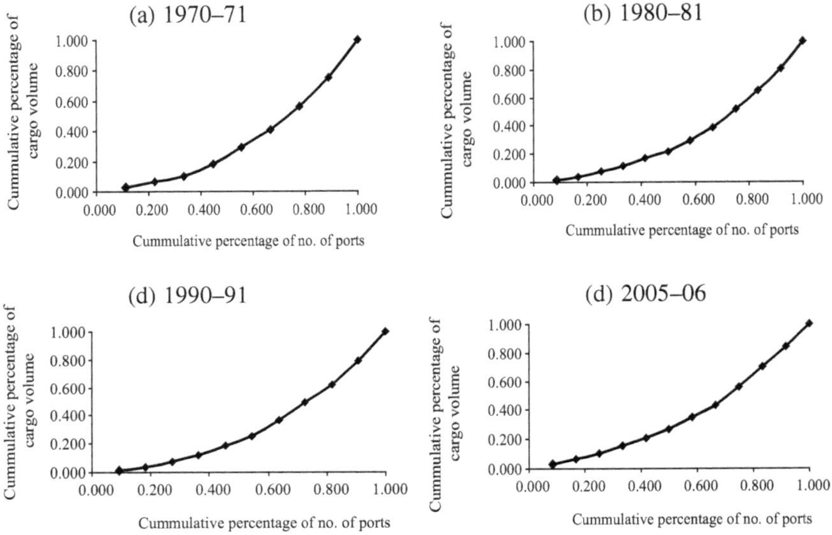

lines and which receives or ships goods through that port' (Weigend, 1958). An alternative hinterland / foreland approach for studying port competition is to look at the degree of traffic concentration in the port system. To assess changes in port system concentration, we have used the Gini coefficient, a widely used index that measures inequality. The Gini coefficient ranges from zero (perfectly even distribution) to one (perfectly concentrated distribution). The level of concentration is shown graphically using a Lorenz curve.[3]

3 Mathematically, the Gini co-efficient is calculated as:

$$G = 0.5 \sum_{i=1}^{n} | X_i - Y_i |$$

where n is the number of ports, X_i is the volume in percent of the i-th port and Y_i is the expected percent if the distribution were perfectly uniform - that is, $Y_i = 1/n$. The relationship between the Gini co-efficient and the Lorenz curve is simple. The Gini co-efficient is equal to the ratio of the area between the Lorenz curve and the diagonal line, relative to the maximum possible area (the entire right angle formed by the bottom and right axes and the diagonal).

Figure 6.1 (a, b, c, d) and Figure 6.2 (a, b, c, d) show the Lorenz curves for 1970–71, 1980–81, 1990–91, and 2005–06, for India's major ports and coastal states respectively for four years. Table 6.2 presents the value of Gini coefficients and Lorenz ratios computed under the two possible combinations - (i) port traffic of major ports, and (ii) combined port traffic of coastal states. In the later case, port traffic considers traffic of both major and minor ports of coastal states. The important findings are spelt out below.

First, port system concentration increased from 0.222 in 1970–71 to 0.291 in 1980–81 for all major ports, which continued more or less unabated until 1990–91 (0.290). But ever since the liberalisation of the Indian economy in 1991, the Gini coefficient drastically declined, (0.204 in 2005–06), even remained at a lower level compared to 1970–71. This is more a reflection of rising import-intensity in all the hinterlands than that of export.

Figure 6.2 Lorenz Curve for Port System of Maritime States

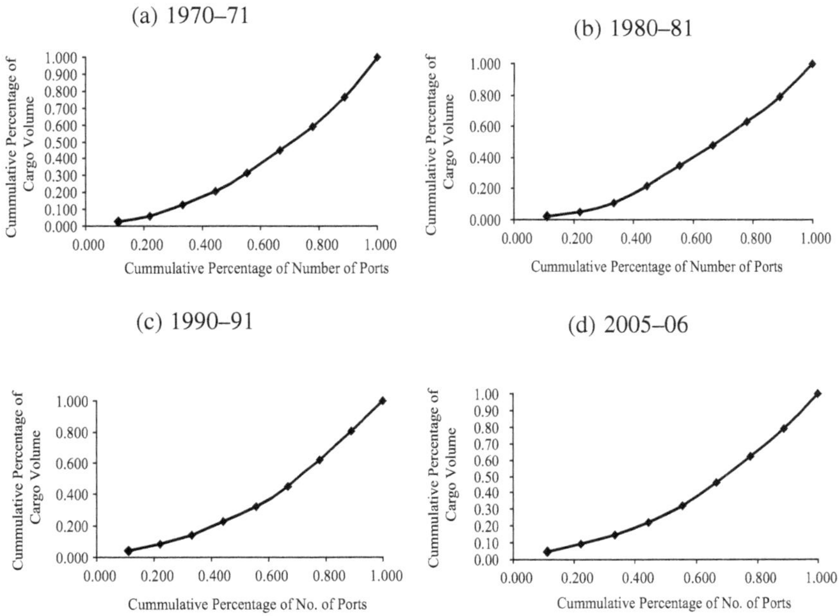

Table 6.2 Lorenz Ratio of Indian Ports

Observations	Lorenz Ratio*				No of Ports / Maritime States			
	1970–71	1980–81	1990–91	2005–06	1970–71	1980–81	1990–91	2005–06
Port Traffic ofMajor Ports	0.356 (0.222)	0.373 (0.291)	0.367 (0.290)	0.295 (0.204)	9	11	12	12
Port Traffic of Maritime States**	0.325 (0.239)	0.300 (0.227)	0.288 (0.232)	0.285 (0.221)	9	9	9	9

Notes:*Numbers in parentheses refer to the Gini Co-efficient. ** Includes both major and minor port traffic

Second, we have found opposite result in case of coastal states. Here, port system concentration has fallen from 0.239 in 1970–71 to 0.221 in 2005–06. Obviously, inclusion of minor port traffic has changed the direction as well as distribution of traffic across the coastal states. In other words, the importance of the minor ports has increased in recent period.

Thus, in the post-liberalisation period, a clear tendency of equalisation with and without minor ports in port system concentration is noticed. One plausible reason for this observation may be that most of the coastal states are trying to utilise minor ports due to limitation of capacity of major ports.

Therefore, in spite of the considerable fluctuation of overseas trade through Indian ports from year to year, one finds a picture of general equalisation of port traffic among the ports of India, particularly in the post-liberalisation period. However, we need to ascertain whether a fall in inequality among Indian ports may mean a rapid rise in the value of commodities handled, or an absolute diversion of traffic away from the larger to the smaller and better equipped ports. We consider here port performance index (PPI), taken from the Chapter 2, across all major ports in order to test whether a fall in port system concentration implies increasing competitiveness in Indian port system.

6.4 Relationship between Port Performance, Cargo Composition and Hinterland's Output

It is generally argued that a rising hinterland / foreland always help the port to sustain its growth. As deemed by this study, we have tried to investigate the factors responsible for the performance of a port. To test this hypothesis, we have used here three independent variables for the year 2005–06- (i) share of overseas port traffic, (ii) port tariff, and (iii) per capita net state domestic product (PCNSDP). This relationship may be captured in equation (6.1).

$$Y = \alpha + \beta X_1 + \gamma X_2 + \delta X_3 + e \tag{6.1}$$

where Y = port performance index, X_1 = port tariff, X_2 = share of overseas traffic, X_3 = PCNSDP, and e = error term. The fitted results of this regression (OLS) are presented in Table 6.3 with corresponding values of the coefficients, t-statistic, Adjusted R^2, DW and F - statistics for the year 2005–06.

The most interesting finding is that port performance is highly contingent upon overseas traffic, the coefficient of which is not only very high (0.196), positive and highly significant (t=2.38). Port tariff and PCNSDP have come out to be insignificant in influencing PPI. The most plausible explanation for lower t-statistics of PCNSDP may be that given the size of the non-coastal states, even a moderate transport network leading to the ports may have sufficient strength to invalidate the attempt at limiting the contour of hinterland to the concerned state only. Hence, the traditional concept of hinterland (which calls forth the use of regional income) needs be modified for successful application to such an analysis. Conversely, this can be taken to imply lower competitive advantage even of a specialised line of production in any region. Therefore, the differential levels of overseas trade are the most influential factor in determining port performance differentials.

6.5 Openness, Port Traffic and Port Capacity

Openness of a country means the degree of its engagement with global trade and economic activity. When a country opens up, it becomes necessary to strengthen its port systems to sustain its international trade. The liberalisation process started in 1991 has enhanced the importance of international trade in the so far closed economy of India. The reforms unleashed India's latent economic potential down the line. India remarkably transformed from a slow growing economy to one of the fastest growing in the world. The trade liberalisation initiated in India in the aftermath of July 1991 has no doubt, led to a perceptible change in

Table 6.3 Regression of PPI on International Traffic, Per Capita Income and Port Tariff

Dependent Variable = PPI

Independent variables	Coefficients	t-statistics	F value	R^2	Adjusted R^2	DW
Constant	3.971	0.722	3.044	0.730	0.654	1.980
Port tariff	0.059	0.019				
International traffic	0.196	2.380				
Per Capita Income (PCNSDP)	0.002	0.493				
No of observations	12					

Notes: 1. All variables are taken for the year 2005–06. 2. Port tariff counts only vessel related charges levied under the Indian Ports Act, 1908 and the Major Port Trust Act, 1963 as other port charges are not comparable. 3. Conversion factor for tariff calculation is taken at US$ 1 = Rs. 42.50

the performance of the external sector. The rapid growth of India's trade, especially in the last decade and a half, represents both a structural change in economy and a marked shift in export orientation. To be precise, share of trade in GDP increased from about 15 percent in 1990 to about 49 percent in 2007 (Government of India, 2009). A large number of policy measures, which were in use for the control of imports, have been dismantled. Also a number of quantitative restrictions, which were imposed in the earlier protectionist regime, have been done away with.

Over time, with greatly reduced barriers to international transactions, Indian participation in the world economy has increased rapidly. Today, with 18 percent per annum growth rate, India's exports crossed US$ 157 billion, while imports increased to US$ 272 billion, grown at about 24 percent per annum since 2000–01 (Table 6.4). India's trade growth in the ongoing decade has been thus highest among all the decades since 1950s. Higher growth in post-1991 period helped India not only to enlarge but also to diversify its exports. Undoubtedly, India has benefited from the globalisation process.

With the liberal measures taken in the post-liberalisation period, Indian ports have been over utilised: 108.75 percent in 1951–52 to 111.27 percent in 2001–02 to 92.85 percent in 2005–06 (Table 6.5). This is specifically true for the ports of Kandla, Mumbai, Chennai, and Vizag that have been continuously suffering from supply-side constraints (i.e., lower capacity) since liberalisation. Beyond the performance indicators so far dealt with, port utilisation depends on the economic characteristics of the hinterland and on the type and modality of transport linkages. Why are some ports over-utilised and others not? The traditional answer is probably a sort of unbalanced growth of manufacturing belts as evolved over time across the country in general and concentration in and around the ports of Kandla, Mumbai, Chennai, and Vizag in particular. As a matter of fact, these are the country's top four ports according to their annual cargo throughput and performance measurement as we have seen in the previous section. Also, these are the ports of four maritime states which contribute higher share in India's manufacturing value added relative to others viz., 14.12 percent, 27.33 percent, 12.17 percent and 7.89 percent respectively in the year 2005–06 (De, 1999).

Table 6.4: India's Merchandise Trade

	Export (US$ billion)	Import (US$ billion)	Total (US$ billion)	Trade in GDP (%)
1950–51	1.27	1.27	2.54	
1960–61	1.35	2.35	3.70	11.77
1970–71	2.03	2.16	4.19	7.76
1980–81	8.49	15.87	24.35	15.56
1990–91	18.15	24.07	42.22	15.48
1995–96	31.80	36.68	68.47	23.13
2000–01	44.56	50.54	95.10	27.38
2001–02	43.83	51.41	95.24	26.38
2002–03	52.72	61.41	114.13	29.92
2003–04	63.84	78.15	141.99	30.78
2004–05	83.54	111.52	195.05	38.22
2005–06	103.09	149.17	252.26	43.61
2006–07	126.26	185.60	311.87	48.78
2007–08	163.13	251.65	414.78	49.38
2008–09	168.70	287.76	456.46	
Annual Average Growth Rates (%)				
1950s	1.10	7.92		
1960s	4.37	–0.52		
1970s	15.63	23.73		
1980s	8.28	4.51		
1990s	9.80	8.46		
2000/01 – 2008/09	18.62	24.90		
1951/52 – 1990/91	7.35	8.91		
1991/92 – 2008/09	13.72	15.77		
1951/52 – 2008/09	9.32	11.04		

Sources: 1. Economic Survey 2007–08, Ministry of Finance, Government of India, based on Director General of Commercial Intelligence and Statistics (DGCIS), Ministry of Commerce and Industry, Government of India. 2. Press Releases on India's Foreign Trade, dated 1 April 2009 and 1 May 2009, New Delhi.

Rise of traffic in Indian ports followed a similar path. It is clear from Table 6.5 that India's international port traffic intensity reached the lowest level of 66.91 percent in 1991–92, and naturally the coastal traffic intensity rate touched the highest level of 33.09 percent in the same year. It is also interesting to note that a fall in international port traffic

Table 6.5 Overview of Port Traffic and Port Capacity of Indian Ports

Year	Port capacity (MT)	International port traffic (MT)	Inland port traffic (MT)	Total port traffic (MT)	Port utilisation rate (%)
1951–52	20.00	17.25	4.50	21.75	108.75
1961–62	36.67	23.83	9.18	33.01	90.02
1971–72	59.55	51.89	7.30	59.19	99.40
1981–82	104.45	72.01	15.97	87.98	84.23
1991–92	169.23	104.81	51.84	156.65	92.57
2001–02	343.95	289.83	92.88	382.71	111.27
2005–06	456.20	333.12	90.45	423.57	92.85
Year	International traffic intensity (%)	Inland traffic intensity (%)	EX-IM Ratio of international port traffic (%)	Openness rate (%)	
1951–52	79.31	20.69	137.75	18	
1961–62	72.19	27.81	120.50	11	
1971–72	87.67	12.33	115.49	9	
1981–82	81.85	18.15	81.02	17	
1991–92	66.91	33.09	74.92	17	
2001–02	75.73	24.27	58.19	22	
2005–06	78.65	21.35	66.99	29	

Notes: 1. Port Utilization Rate = (Port Traffic / Port Capacity)* 100. 2. International Traffic Intensity = (International Traffic / Total Traffic)*100. 3. Inland Traffic Intensity = (Inland Traffic / Total Traffic)*100. 4. Openness Rate = [(Exports + Imports) / GDP] *100, taken at US$ term.

Source: Ministry of Shipping, Road Transport and Highways, Government of India

intensity means a rise in inland (coastal) traffic intensity that is shown in an interval of 10 years from 1951–52 to 2005–06. This means that during the lean period of international trade, port systems had been used for inland trade. Although Indian ports handled 4.50 million tonnes of inland cargo in 1951–52, which at the end of 2005–06 became 90.45 million tonnes, inland traffic intensity of all the major ports except Kandla has grown faster than international traffic intensity in the post-liberalisation period. While this has reduced the burden on overland transportation, port infrastructure has failed to exert its favourable impact on export competitiveness due mainly to capacity constraints and poor performance. The output per-ship-berth-day and ship turn-around-time at major ports have worsened in the post-liberalisation period. The situation is more aggravated in case of old ports like Kolkata where average turnaround time of 4.12 days is really a serious concern. Likewise, its 77 percent capacity utilisation is extremely low compared to the all India average of 93 percent. The situation appears much grave when one considers costs. It is 40 percent cheaper to ship from Singapore to Mumbai than from Singapore to Kolkata. Given that international ship turn-around times range between 3 to 10 hours rather than a week or more, it becomes very clear why the capacity utilisation of Kolkata port is so low. Beyond the proximate causes, declining water draft and the riverine nature may be the two main factors for the lower values of the performance indicators of Kolkata port.

Again, during the last five and a half decades, Indian ports are becoming more and more engaged not only in imports but also in inland traffic. It can be noted from Table 6.5 that the export-import ratio of international port traffic has fallen from 137.75 percent in 1951–52 to 66.99 percent in 2005–06. This is a direct reflection of our rising trade deficit. Some emerging trends of a hitherto semi-closed economy are obvious from Table 6.5.

First, shortfall in port capacity will be a glaring concern in the coming years as liberalisation gains further momentum incorporating the agricultural sector also; in 2005–06 port traffic was 423.57 million tonnes against the capacity of 456.20 million tonnes.

Second, increasing trade orientation (openness) has halted the fast rate of growth of inland traffic since 1991. For example, inland traffic has grown at an average annual rate of 26.30 percent from 1951–52 to 1991–92, while international traffic has grown by 12.69 percent per annum. This trend has completely reversed after 1991. Although international traffic has been rising at approximately the same rate (11.79 percent) since 1991, that of inland traffic has fallen to 4.41 percent. While this is certainly an encouraging symptom from the viewpoint of the country's openness, but the export intensity of international traffic has been declining at faster rate in the post-reform period (5.93 percent per annum during 1991–92 to 2005–06 as against 1.14 percent per annum during 1951–52 to 1991–92). This means that a larger import passed through overburdened ports of India with a rising magnitude of openness.

6.6 Port Reform and Concentration of Private Terminal Operators in India

After many years of inconclusive deliberations, the Government of India finally took steps to invite private capital in running port facilities on BOT basis in late 1990s. In July 1997, Jawaharlal Nehru Port Trust (JNPT) signed a 30-year concession agreement with Nava Sheva International Container Terminal Ltd. (NSICT), a DPI-led consortium, to build, operate and transfer (BOT) a container terminal. This was India's first port privatisation programme. Since then concession agreements signed at Jawaharlal Nehru, Chennai, Cochin, Vizag, Kandla, Kolkata, Mumbai and Tuticorin ports for container terminals. In case of minor ports, although several ports are being operated by the private sector such as Mundra, Pipavav, Kakinada, Gangavaram, and Krishnapatnam, we find private terminal operators are running container terminals at Mundra and Pipavav only.

A decade after the port reform initiated through Jawaharlal Nehru Port, India's coast is now dotted with many private terminal operators. Today, almost 90 percent of India's container traffic is handled by the private sector (Table 6.6), of which two private terminals at the Jawaharlal Nehru Port together handle about 56 percent. The private terminal operators' engagement in Indian ports has not always been through direct concession with the port authorities, but is also through strategic acquisitions such as buying majority stakes in Kolkata and Kandla container terminals by PSA from ABG Industries and DPI's acquisition of P&O Ports and subsequent control of major container terminals in India. This however had led to an explicit rise in concentration of private terminal operators in Indian port sector, which is nonetheless showing sort of an oligopolistic nature of port operation.

While the global container industry remains highly fragmented (UNCTAD, 2008), Indian container port industry is highly concentrated in some selected ports. As Table 6.6 shows, it is dominated by a single firm (say, DPI). We use the Herfindahl-Hirschman Index (HHI) to measure market concentration for purposes of antitrust (anti-competitive) behaviour of terminal operators.[4] From Table 6.7, it can be seen that the Herfindahl-Hirschman Index, an indicator of market concentration, is at 2056.34, where 1000 indicates concentrated and 1800 highly concentrated. It potentially raises significant competitive concerns because total HHI score has crossed the 1800 mark since 2006–07 (Table 6.7).

4 The HHI's development (Herfindahl, 1950) is attributed to two noted economists, namely, Orris C. Herfindahl, who developed it as part of his doctoral dissertation, 'Concentration in the Steel Industry' at Columbia University, New York, in 1950, as well as noted economist Albert O. Hirschman, who used it in his research in industry concentration in 1950. There are several complex models available that are intended to reflect market behaviour (e.g. Cournot and Bertrand models and their derivatives), but their roots are embedded in the general concepts of market concentration and firm dominance. See, Cournot (1927) and Bertrand (1883). HHI is calculated as:

$$H_{it} = \sum_{i=1}^{n} \left(\frac{x_{it}}{X_{it}} \right)^2$$

where H_{it} is value of concentration index for terminal i for the year t, x_{it} denotes the container traffic of terminal i in year t, X_{it} means total container port traffic in year t.

Table 6.6 Share of Private Container Terminals of Container Traffic in India

(%)

Terminal (Operator)	Port	2000–01	2001–02	2002–03	2003–04	2004–05	2005–06	2006–07	2007–08
NSICT (DPW)	Jawaharlal Nehru	28.13	31.34	30.09	28.87	26.91	28.19	31.03	33.63
GTICT (APM)	Jawaharlal Nehru							21.30	22.17
CCT (DPW)	Chennai	14.25	11.92	12.63	13.36	13.26	13.07	17.95	18.19
TCT (PSA)	Tuticorin	6.36	7.40	6.33	6.29	6.71	6.17	7.13	6.65
MICT (DPW)	Mundra				1.26	4.81	4.61	5.11	5.15
IGT (DPW)	Cochin	5.79	5.26	4.92	4.21	4.04	3.90	4.05	3.71
KCIT (PSA)	Kandla							3.21	2.44
VCT (DPW)	Vizag				0.51	0.99	2.10	2.25	2.17
KCT (PSA)	Kolkata						1.82	2.10	2.22
PCT (APM)	Pipavav				1.54	1.78	1.69	1.76	1.60

Note: DPW – Dubai Port World, APM – A P Moller (Maersk), PSA – Port of Singapore Authority
Source: Author's own collection based on field visit to individual port.

Table 6.7 Concentration of Private Terminal Operators: HHI Scores

Terminal	Operator	2000–01	2001–02	2002–03	2003–04	2004–05	2005–06	2006–07	2007–08
NSICT	DPW	791.50	982.20	905.11	833.59	724.33	794.65	1025.75	1131.17
CCT	DPW	203.09	142.18	159.42	178.57	175.89	170.93	359.09	331.02
IGT	DPW	33.52	27.70	24.23	17.76	16.35	15.24	16.37	13.77
MICT	DPW				1.58	23.11	21.27	26.11	26.54
VCT	DPW				0.26	0.99	4.42	5.06	4.72
TCT	PSA	40.39	54.77	40.02	39.62	45.03	38.08	66.07	44.21
KICT	PSA							10.32	5.96
KCT	PSA						3.30	4.41	4.94
PCT	APM				2.37	3.18	2.86	3.10	2.55
GTI	APM							542.73	491.46
India		1068.50	1206.84	1128.76	1073.75	988.89	1050.74	2059.02	2056.34

Figure 6.3 Trends in HHI of Private Container Terminal Operators

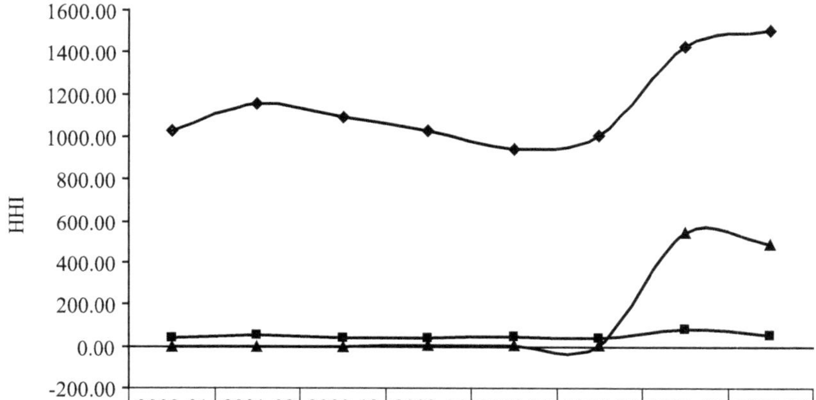

	2000-01	2001-02	2002-03	2003-04	2004-05	2005-06	2006-07	2007-08
DP World	1028.11	1152.07	1088.76	1031.76	940.67	1006.50	1432.39	1507.22
PSA	40.39	54.77	40.02	39.62	45.03	41.38	80.80	55.11
APM	0.00	0.00	0.00	2.37	3.18	2.86	545.83	494.01

Therefore, HHI scores indicate an increasing degree of concentration in the Indian container port sector.

However, disaggregating the HHI in terms of terminal operators, we get concentration scores for each private terminal operator. Figure 6.3 shows that with HHI score of 1507.22 in 2007–08, DPI (DP World) has captured the majority share of the Indian container port industry. The DP World's HHI score has not only been very high but has also increased from 1028.11 in 2000–01.

Concentration is relatively high in those ports which have higher TFP (Total Factor Productivity) growth and show a unidirectional causal relationship from performance to traffic (Table 6.8). For example, Jawaharlal Nehru Port which has not only attained highest TFP growth amonst all the major ports in India during the period 1980–81 to 2005–06 (0.21), but has also scored highest in concentration (HHI score of 1501). Chennai, Tuticorin and Vizag come next in that order. Having said that, the most important message we want to convey is that the

Table 6.8. Productivity and Competition: TFP and HHI

Port	Causal Relationship[1]	Total Factor Productivity (TFP) Growth[2]	Terminal Operator's Share in Indian Container Traffic[3] (%)	HHI Score[3]
		1980–01 to 2005–06	2005–06 to 2007–08	
Jawaharlal Nehru	Performance → Traffic	0.2084	52.685	1500.95
New Mangalore	*	0.1456		
Paradip	*	0.1286		
Chennai	Performance → Traffic	0.1026	16.403	287.01
Haldia	Performance ↔ Traffic	0.0851		
Vizag	Performance → Traffic	0.0793	2.173	4.73
Tuticorin	Performance → Traffic	0.0752	6.650	49.45
Cochin	Performance → Traffic	0.067	3.887	15.13
Kandla	Performance → Traffic	0.0622	2.825	8.14
Mumbai	Performance → Traffic	0.0322		
Mormugao	*	0.0292		
Kolkata	Performance → Traffic	-0.0305	2.047	4.22

Notes: 1. Refer Table 3.4. 2. Refer Table 4.2. 3. Period average. *No causal relationship.

potential for oligopolistic behaviour remains in the private container terminal industry. In a sense, the Indian government has miserably failed to control the rise of private monopolies in the container port industry.

The aforesaid findings have following two important policy lessons:

First, since the advancement in technology has attracted new capital through both public and private sectors in Indian ports, rise of concentration in Indian ports at the present moment is a mere natural outcome when the market is not properly regulated. Hence, government has to ensure competition in the Indian port sector, which is essential for the long run sustainability of Indian ports.

Second, ideally intra- and inter- port competition should be more where TFP growth is high. So far, it did not occur in India. As a result, a few giant terminal operators are fast capturing the market through horizontal merger, which is thus working against the competitive nature of the market and the globalisation process. The benefits of TFP appear to be wiped out by the lax of regulation.

The interest in the Indian container port system concentration stems from the fear that a few giant operators may not be inhibited from entering each other's market. Some type of collusive arrangements may also rise. The arrangement may be an outright market sharing agreement that moderates competition—and it could work against globalisation. Our task shall necessarily be to keep the system competitive. The challenge is thus to introduce better governance and competition in the port sector so that it ultimately leads to sustain higher productivity and efficiency. We need to allow market forces work by encouraging competition through the correct strategies and avoid strict regulation (e.g. imposing tariffs). We know from experience today that we can have fierce port operator competition with only a very few rivals - Seattle and Tacoma, Singapore and Hong Kong, Rotterdam and Amsterdam. So, there is no need to assume that Indian ports behave anti-competitively. Instead, we should monitor the competitive behaviour of the terminal operators and also the ports where the government has adopted to landlord port model.

6.7 Public Investment and Regulation

A review of literature broadly suggests that three types of models have been adopted across the world for privatisation for port system (Baird, 1997). In the first model, only the port operation part is transferred to efficient private sector. This type of arrangement is referred to as a 'landlord' or 'tool' port. In this model, port land is still in public ownership, and regulatory activities are also the responsibility of the government. There are many examples of this type of arrangement, especially throughout North American and European ports, in which terminals are generally leased to the private sector. In the second model, two elements like port operation and property rights are controlled by the private sector. In this case, government controls the regulatory matters and the conservancy of navigable approach channels. In UK, ports like Tilbury, Felixstowe and Harwich and ports of Australia are owned and operated by the private sector. In the third model, all the three powers - regulatory, land ownership and operation - become the responsibility of the private sector. With this, government virtually does not have any role except to react in certain cases like pollution, accidents and threat to the sovereignty of the country. Three of the top 100 container ports, Southampton, Liverpool and Thamesport (all are in UK) conform to this model. There are also examples of general cargo ports (not specialised in container) which also belong to this category. Baird (1997) has shown that out of 100 top container ports in the world, seven ports are still managed by government (mainly ports in South Africa, India, Israel and Singapore), 88 ports belong to first model, two ports conform to second model and three ports belong to third model.

Alternatively, a joint venture between public and private sector splits the costs and risks of a new port development, and this appears to be one of the main approaches currently used for port investment in China. Clearly, these privatisation methods can help facilitate an advanced port system whilst minimising state expenditure, and without any need to transfer ultimate property rights or regulatory control from the public sector.

Inefficient ports, whether through lack of integrated transport network, outdated work practices and, obsolete facilities, can stall economic development. This is one of the main reasons why local governments are actively seeking private sector participation in their port sector usually via lease, concession, BOT (build, operate and transfer), or joint venture arrangements. There is also a need to introduce efficiency and know-how of the private sector. Increasing specialisation and standardisation in the shipping and transport industry have resulted in the formation of expert multinational terminal operating companies, often subsidiaries of shipping lines, who know precisely how to meet the ever changing, and increasingly demanding needs of ports users. These firms benefit from economies of scale and learning through their wide geographic scope of activities which make them fully aware of the best practice industry on a global basis.

There is also pressure to reduce demands on the public sector budget but this does not necessarily mean that the government withdraws entirely form investing in its ports. Many examples of the first model demonstrate that the state may continue to be responsible for provision of new infrastructure but that the private sector provides the superstructure such as cranes and terminal buildings. This is more a partnership approach in which the government still retains at least some degree of control over its ports industry. Even in BOT arrangements the government will generally retain its public port authority, may also impose restrictions on future tariff increases, share in port profits, stipulate minimum throughput targets, and property rights which ultimately revert to the government at the end of the contract period.

The reasons for the slowdown in Indian port development are many. One of the main reasons is the low Plan investments in the transport sector as whole, and only a very insignificant part of it has been devoted to port sector over the half century after independence. It is clear from Table 6.9 that the share of the transport sector in total plan outlay has fallen from 22.10 percent during the 1st Five Year Plan (FYP) to 23.50 percent during the 2nd FYP to 16.77 percent in the 10th FYP. Moreover, the share of ports in the transport sector has all the more static in last five decades or so. It is surprising to note that such a crucial infrastructure facility like port is the worst affected area in terms of both allocation and utilisation of development fund during the last ten Plans. Again, in all the Plans except the Fourth FYP, fund utilisation in port sector has always been marred by inefficiency. Failure to utilise the disbursed fund may have been responsible for reduced allocation in the subsequent period. And as a matter of fact, due to this low investment adequate capacity has not been created. In fact, the government has failed to understand the crucial role the port sector can play in the liberal economic regime. But this sort of reasoning can not go beyond the proximate explanation. The more fundamental cause must be sought in the lack of export orientation of our investment policies starting from the Second Plan to the Ninth Plan. This is

Table 6.9 Five Year Plan (FYP) Allocations in Transport Sector in India

	1st FYP 1951–56	2nd FYP 1956–61	3rd FYP 1961–66	4th FYP 1969–74	5th FYP 1974–79	6th FYP 1980–85	7th FYP 1985–90	8th FYP 1992–97	9th FYP 1997–02	10th FYP 2002–07
Ports and Shipping										
FUR (%)	75.68	73.33	60.78	127.69	85.46	112.06	123.01	64.72	51.87	61.03
STTSPO (%)	7.31	3.46	10.97	7.58	10.54	5.36	5.43	6.34	12.03	7.02
Road and Road Transportation										
FUR (%)	108.89	92.02	148.15	98.97	125.72	113.03	121.83	125.42	183.75	121.76
STTSPO (%)	26.68	20.25	21.29	33.88	24.96	28.47	22.96	22.88	10.86	56.44
Railway										
FUR (%)	81.27	80.33	148.99	88.95	93.69	129.12	134.17	118.75	102.18	113.24
STTSPO (%)	52.77	69.28	63.80	40.84	40.63	42.22	54.47	48.50	55.67	28.69
Civil Aviation										
FUR (%)	79.31	113.95	89.09	87.19	87.24	111.41	256.99	177.54	59.39	89.32
STTSPO (%)	5.73	3.31	3.94	7.90	6.22	7.11	3.35	7.28	13.62	6.29
Total transport										
FUR (%)	85.77	84.68	142.15	98.09	102.27	115.57	130.17	115.78	94.45	110.23
STPO (%)	22.10	23.50	23.10	16.00	14.10	12.80	13.50	13.10	14.23	16.77

Notes: 1. Plan outlay considers both Central and State Plan Outlays. 2. Road sector does not include allocation made for road transport sector. 3. Port sector does not include allocation made for shipping, IWT, Lighthouse and Lightships. 4. FUR means Fund Utilisation Rate (= Plan Expenditures / Plan Outlay). 5. STTSPO means Share in Total Transport Sector Plan Outlay.

Source: Planning Commission, Government of India

more so for a country where ports account for more than 80 percent of merchandise trade.

Apart from low plan investments, awareness, direction and understanding of the port industry has been lacking which could motivate the port authorities about the efficacy of both revenue earning and catalytic role of port. There is an urgent need for a coordinated policy for regulating and encouraging investments from both public and private sectors in ports. One may be surprised to note that although all the 13 major ports are controlled by the Government of India, the Government still does not have a coordinated port policy. It has only some guidelines issued from time to time on ad hoc basis. Again, some of the maritime states like Gujarat and Maharashtra have some port policies of their own but they also lack the required direction (De, 2003). There is no doubt that the country needs an atmosphere for an all out investments for ushering into a commercial revolution in the port industry. But to do these Indian ports need to go through a process of technological development which demands such monetary and fiscal policies, which are no short of a revolution.

Although central government and its respective maritime states have opened the sector for private investments but experiences suggest that investors face strong bureaucracy in getting the projects cleared. The major trouble is that quite a large number of clearances are required which are controlled by both central and state governments. And there is lack of transparency beyond of course the strategic nature of this sector.

Another very critical factor that has accounted for poor performance in India's waterfront industry is the absence of inter-port competition, which has been the source of substantial productivity increases in national port systems in many countries. Shielding the domestic ports against competitive pressures as a matter of government policy is now a legacy that is hard to overcome.

Apart from all micro level incongruities, in India, cargo and vessel handling charges are responsible for distorting the inter-port competitive environment. Look at Table 6.10 for port tariff of major ports of India for the years 2001–02 and 2005–06. It is reasonably true that port tariff motivates the cargo flow. In India, port tariff is a combination of

Table 6.10 Port Tariff of the Major Ports of India: 2005–06

Ports	Vessel Tariff		Cargo Tariff	
	2001–02	2005–06	2001–02	2005–06
	US$ / GRT		US$ / TEU	
Kandla	0.47	0.73	62.10	88.57
Mumbai	0.41	0.82	68.49	82.81
Jawaharlal Nehru	0.44	0.51	55.88	62.18
Mormugao	0.52	0.83	29.06	47.33
New Mangalore	0.48	0.96	38.27	43.15
Cochin	0.56	0.83	48.90	56.86
Tuticorin	0.48	0.59	31.72	48.56
Chennai	0.51	0.63	47.55	51.65
Vizag	0.62	0.68	56.30	67.09
Paradip	0.72	0.75	25.42	29.58
Kolkata	0.83	0.91	92.39	133.10
Haldia	0.83	0.91	75.11	97.62

Notes: 1. Tariff rate includes port dues, pilotage, towage, anchorage and berth hire charges levied on foreign vessels for single entry to the port only. 2. Cargo tariff applies only to container box.
Source: Calculated based on Scale of Rates of Major Ports of India, TAMP, Ministry of Shipping, Road Transport and Highways, Government of India.

cargo related charges and vessel related charges - those levied under the Indian Ports Act, 1908 and Major Port Trusts Act, 1963. From Table 6.10, one may have noticed that west coast ports have lower vessel related tariff than those of east coast ports, while east coast ports have lower cargo related charges (applicable to container traffic only) than west coast ports.[5] It is sometimes argued that annual incidence of intrinsically avoidable costs to the Indian economy occasioned by considerable demurrage charges, the extra expenditures of transhipment, con-

5 The way port tariff is simplified here should not be stretched too far to make any rigorous conclusion. In fact there are numerous rates of tariff levied on various items. Naturally therefore, we have here considered only the vessel related charges as levied under Indian Ports Act, 1908 and the Major Port Trust Act, 1963. Other charges are not easily comparable.

gestion of ship and cargo handling installations could be as high as US$ 1.5 billion (IDFC, 2001). Moreover, the country's importers and exporters generally forego the ability to count on now universally common 'fixed-day-of-the-week' services offered by the international liner industry in response to the spreading practice of selling and buying on a 'just-in-time' basis. Because of uncertainties in the speed of cargo handling and the availability of transport services India's traders and producers are forced to conduct their business with substantial buffer stocks. While no official estimates of the annual cost incidence related to such hedging are available, it may not be very illogical if one puts it at several billion dollars.

The consequences of all these shortcomings for the Indian economy continue to be severe. In the liner trades very few carriers serve India's ports through direct calls. Because of the high costs of operation of modern deep-sea line haul tonnage carriers cannot accept the long waiting times at Indian ports. Most general cargo traffic, particularly container traffic, takes place through transhipment at Colombo, Dubai, or Singapore. The extra transit times and additional costs incurred by Indian importers and exporters are substantial. The costs of excessive ship waiting times in ports due to slow cargo processing in the case of bulk trades are passed on to the ultimate user thereby raising the price of imports unnecessarily and undermining the competitiveness of Indian exports in the international markets.

6.8 Conclusions

The study of the consanguinity between economics and geographical factors is unavoidable for explaining the ultimate economic reality. Both the classical economists and the pioneers of development economics recognised this. This study is concerned with the economics of Indian ports as one important phenomenon in Indian economic geography, and its relationship with regional development under free market economy.

Although inter-port competition has been rising since 1991, the performance of the west coast ports appears to be better than those of the east coast. Moreover, overseas traffic intensity is found to be the most significant determinant of port performance index derived with the help of principal component analysis from eight individual port performance indicators. Finally, given the fact that port is the most neglected sector over six decades of planning, with increasing openness absence of an integrated policy toward export transport network has resulted in declining export intensity, and rising domestic coastal traffic in Indian ports.

Let us briefly summarise the major findings of the chapter. First, declining inequality among Indian ports has failed to strengthen the country's port sector. Geographically, the ports of eastern India have stagnated, while the same in west and south coasts have flourished. Second, contrary to conventional belief, performance of a port has been proved to be significantly dependent upon overseas cargo. Third, there has been a strong rise of market concentration in port sector, and few private terminal operators show anti-competitive practices. Fourth, in the absence of an integrated policy of manufacturing belt, transport network and export orientation, existing capacity of the ports is being utilised for domestic coastal trade and imports. Fifth, allocations of funds by both central and state governments over the Plan periods are found to be too low to utilise the potential of India's huge coastline through development of transport infrastructure.

These findings have very important policy implications for future development of Indian ports. In this light, further research becomes imminent in order to see to what extent such non-price factor as port is responsible for our deluding export performance. Further study must be undertaken to see whether rising imports through Indian ports is a barrier to Indian export when there is capacity constraint. Given that export consignment is always contingent upon timely supply, if the port authorities do not have any special incentives for export shipment, they can not but use the existing capacity for import traffic only. Moreover, in such an endeavour, serious attention must be focussed on the origin and destination of the cargo composition before any full-fledged policy initiative for future investment in port development is undertaken. Another major limitation of the present study is its failure to incorporate the necessary transport linkage between the port, manufacturing belt, and the hinterland.

The findings presented herein are revisionist, and highly aggregative. The methods and data used are likely to come under closer scrutiny for future studies will no doubt refine and revise our arguments. First, other theoretical approaches might be explored. New ways of thinking about growth could provide other models in which geographic dynamics and economic growth could be assessed jointly. Second, as further advances in the growth literature define the steady state more effectively, the robustness of our results can be tested, and the analysis extended. Third, considering the mode of transport linkage with the ports one should also examine the effectiveness of the economics of ports not only for practical implementation of the thrust area of liberalisation (that is to raise export) but also for spreading India's halted urbanisation. Fourth, a detailed study on origin and destination of port traffic is necessary for better understanding of the economics of Indian port. For this, the study of such an inseparable eco-geographical phenomenon must be brought to the forefront of Indian economic analysis.

Summary and Policy Implications

7.1 Summary

This book attempts at understanding empirically the process of India's port sector development in terms of some broad attributes of performance in the context of globalisation. In other words, the book tries to quantitatively evaluate the structural metamorphosis in Indian port sector covering a period which formally starts after a quarter century of planning for industrialisation, and ends up in the post-liberalisation era. The main emphasis of the book is on performance evaluation, technological change, labour productivity, total factor productivity growth and market concentration. This is an empirical study dealing with published government data on Indian major ports and covering a period of last two decades and a half starting from 1980–81.

It is clear from the examination contained in this book that rapid and profound changes are occurring in Indian ports. Overreaching all the themes in the foregoing chapters is that good performance is the key to sustain productivity and efficiency.

The first theme presents performance of Indian ports. The analysis carried out in this book shows that performance does lead to increased traffic. The estimated elasticity of port traffic with respect to port performance indicates that every 10 percent increase of performance causes 6 percent higher traffic. If a port performs better by improving its operational and asset performance indicators initially then it is going to attract higher traffic, whereas an efficient management can lead to significant increases in port traffic, which may then increase the demand for port services. The issue of causality between performance and traffic in Indian ports has also been dealt explicitly. The analysis of this volume shows that the relatively larger ports like Kandla, Mumbai, Chennai, Vizag support the hypothesis that performance causes traffic. We therefore suggest that efforts to adopt performance augmenting technologies or performance improvement measurements will certainly have some positive influence on port traffic. Interestingly, no port confirms the reverse hypothesis, i.e. traffic causes performance.

The second underlying theme refers to the total factor productivity (TFP) growth in Indian ports. This study shows that Indian ports are becoming more capital intensive in the post-liberalisation period. Except Kolkata, rest Indian ports have come out with statistically significant TFP changes over the period of two decades and a half starting since 1980–81. The only port, which has registered negative TFP change during the whole period, is Kolkata port. At the same time, none of the Indian ports has recorded statistically significant positive TFP change in the post-liberalisation (post-1991) period. However, New Mangalore port has achieved statistically significant negative TFP change in the post-liberalisation period. This clearly indicates that economic climate in India in post-1991 period has not made any substantial impact on the performance of Indian ports in terms of the most popular measure of performance, TFP. The economic climate of the country appears to have remained largely unchanged in terms of TFP performance among Indian ports during the post-reform period.

The third important theme refers to the technological change in terms of its power and ability to improve the productivity of labour in Indian port sector. Analysis carried out in this book indicates that there has been an upward shift of the productivity locus in Indian ports, which implies that the Indian ports have witnessed some kind of technological metamorphosis in the last two decades and a half starting since 1980–81. Hence, these findings have important implications for technology policy in the port sector in LDCs and particularly in India.

The fourth theme has dealt with inequality of Indian ports. This book shows that the ports of eastern India have stagnated, while the same located in west and south coasts have flourished. Allocation of funds by both central and state governments over the Plan periods has been found to be too low to utilise the potential of India's huge coastline through development of port infrastructure.

A fifth – and possibly the single most powerful – theme relates to the competitive environment of Indian port sector. This volume shows that there has been a strong rise of market concentration in port sector. Ideally, TFP and competition in port move in parallel. A port with higher TFP witnesses higher intra-port competition and vice versa. But, it did not occur in India so far. The potential for oligopolistic behaviour remains in the private container terminal industry. As a result, a few giant terminal operators are fast capturing the market, which is thus working against the competitive nature of the market and the globalisation process. The benefit of TFP is thus appeared to be wiped out due to the lax of regulation. In a sense, the government has failed to control the rise of private monopolies in the container port industry. Therefore, the government has to ensure a competitive market, which is essential for long run sustainability of the Indian ports.

The interest in the Indian container port system concentration stems from the fear that a few giant operators may not be inhibited from entering each other's market. Some type of collusive arrangements may also rise. The arrangement may be an outright market sharing agreement that moderates competition – and it could work against globalisation. Our task shall necessarily be to keep the system competitive. The challenge is thus to introduce better governance , institution and policy for the port sector so that it ultimately leads to sustain higher productivity and efficiency. At the same time, we need to let market forces work by encouraging competition through the correct strategies and avoid strict regulation (e.g. imposing tariffs). We know from experience today that we can have fierce port operator competition with only a very few rivals – Seattle and Tacoma, Singapore and Hong Kong, Rotterdam and Amsterdam. So, there is no need to assume that Indian ports behave anti-competitively. Instead, we should monitor the competitive behaviour of the terminal operators and also the ports where the government ownership has transformed into landlord port model.

7.2 Implications for Future Research

This study is an attempt to understand the role of ports in India's economic development in terms of general economic attributes. In analysing the above objective, this work has provided lesser comprehensive coverage to a number of important economic issues, which can be covered in future studies. Some of these areas for further extensions are as follows.

First, we have not considered here the spatial concentration of manufacturing activities in and around the ports, differential geographical attributes, logistics networks, and differential nation-wide infrastructure stocks associated with each region which may have very substantial bearings on port traffic. The findings of this volume may be further substantiated incorporating these exogenous factors.

Second, implications of this book might have been stronger if some external factors which have direct bearings on port traffic and performance like depth of the navigational channel, nature of shipping routes and vessel sizes, level of technologically advanced equipment, etc. were considered.

Third, given the aggregate nature of the performance index, there might be some potential for obtaining biased results.

Fourth, Granger causality test considers long time period properties preferably panel data. For this reason, conclusions obtained in this book are subject to revision if conducted by tests based on a larger period.

Fifth, future work can be attempted to measure causal relationship between cargo-specific performance and traffic for each port and then perform the procedures as described in this book. The reason for this is that most of the Indian ports are designed to handle specific categories of cargo which have declined over time while other types of traffic have gained importance. But the port's berth configurations have not yet adjusted to the new categories of cargo. In this backdrop, such an analysis can lead to distinct results for each cargo baskets in each port.

Sixth, productivity of a port is the resultant of a nation's overall infrastructure networks including road, rail, electricity, housing, banking, postal and telecommunication facilities, demographic condition, irrigation facility, openness, labour unrest, macro-economic stability (e.g. inflation and foreign exchange rates) and the like. A long period causality test with aggregate productivity as well as public and private infrastructure capital for Indian ports are required for understanding the role of port in a comparable framework.

Seventh, there has been tremendous spurt in international research on the relationship between globalisation and productivity through either (i) a bias towards skilled worker, or (ii) application of higher technology, or both. If only the first factor is in operation then there is a potential danger of rising unemployment and wage differential against the unskilled worker which doubtless represent a larger share of the labour force in Indian port sector. If only the second factor is in operation then ports having lower rate of capital accumulation (representing lower technological adaptation) will find it increasingly difficult to compete in a global market. Apart from the above, there might be differing impact on ports having inherently different labour-intensity and hence on the emerging nature of unemployment. Therefore, further study should be undertaken at much disaggregated level of classification.

Eighth, since the findings of this study have very important policy implications for future development of Indian ports, further research becomes imminent in order to see to what extent such non-price factor as port is responsible for our deluding export performance.

Ninth, other theoretical approaches might be explored. New ways of thinking about growth could provide other models in which geographic dynamics and economic growth could be assessed jointly.

Tenth, as further advances in the growth literature define the steady state more effectively, the robustness of our results can be tested, and the analysis extended.

Eleventh, considering the mode of transport linkage with the ports one should also examine the effectiveness of the economics of ports not only for practical implementation of the thrust area of liberalisation (that is to raise export) but also for spreading India's halted urbanisation.

Twelfth, a detailed study on origin and destination of port traffic is necessary for better understanding of the economics of Indian port. For this, the study of such an inseparable eco-geographical phenomenon must be brought to the forefront of Indian economic analysis.

Thirteenth, if the government is to rely increasingly on the private sector, then it is the competition which can make the private sector efficient. There are many examples of private sector inefficiency caused by a lack of competition as well as by archaic rules and regulations and excessive bureaucracy. Therefore, further studies are needed to understand the complex relationship between competition, ownership, and performance in Indian ports. The outcomes of this study might help the government not only to effectively regulate the private sector but also to motivate all the stakeholders in the port industry to carry on their own work more efficiently.

Bibliography

Abramovitz, M. (1956). "Resource and Output Trends in the United States since 1870", *American Economic Review*, Vol. 46, No. 2, pp. 5–23.

Ahluwalia, I. J. (1991). *Productivity and Growth in Indian Manufacturing*, Oxford University Press, New Delhi.

Aschauer, D. A. (1989). "Is Public Expenditure Productive?" *Journal of Monetary Economics*, Vol. 23, No. 1, pp. 177–200.

Baird, A. (1997). "Privatization Defined: Is it the Universal Panacea?", Transportation, Water and Urban Development Department, The World Bank, Washington, D.C.

Bannerjee, A., Dolado, J., Galbraith, J. and Hendry, D. (1993). *Co-integration, Error-Correction, and the Economic Analysis of Non-stationary Data*, Oxford University Press, London

Bardhan, P. and Mookherjee, D. (1998). "Expenditure Decentralization and the Delivery of Public Services in Developing Countries", Working Paper No. C98–104, Centre for International and Development Economics Research, University of California, Berkeley.

Barro, R. and Sala-i-Martin, X. (1995). *Economic Growth*, McGraw Hill, New York.

Bauer, P. W. (1990). "Decomposing TFP Growth in the Presence of Cost Inefficiency, Nonconstant Returns to Scale, and Technological Progress", *Journal of Productivity Analysis*, Vol. 1, pp. 287–299.

Bertrand, J. (1883). "Theorie Mathematique de la Richesse Social" (loosely translated as Mathematical Theory of Social Welfare), *Journal des Savants*, pp. 499–508.

Binswanger, H. P., S. R. Khandkur, and Rosenzweig, M. R. (1989). "How Infrastructure and Financial Institutions affect Agriculture Output and Investment in India", Policy Planning and Research Working Paper No. 163, Latin America and the Caribbean Country Department II, The World Bank, Washington, D. C.

Bollard, A. and Pickford, M. (1998). "Deregulation and Competition Policy in the Transport Sector in New Zealand", *Journal of Transport Economics and Policy*, Vol. 32, pp. 267–276.

Case, K.E. and Fair, R. C. (1999). *Principles of Economics*, Prentice Hall, New Jersey.

Caves, D. W., Christensen, L. R. and Tretheway, M. W. (1984). "Economics of Density versus Economics of Scale: Why Trunk and Local Service Airline Costs Differ", *Rand Journal of Economics*, Vol. 15, pp. 471–489.

Chung, K. C. (1993). "Port Performance Indicators", Working Paper No. PS–6, Transportation, Water and Urban Development Department, The World Bank, Washington, D.C.

Clark, X., Dollar, D. and Micco, A. (2004). "Port Efficiency, Maritime Transport Costs and Bilateral Trade", Working Paper 10353, NBER, Cambridge.

Coelli, T., Prasada Rao, D. S. and Battese, G. E. (1998). *An Introduction to Efficiency and Productivity Analysis*, Kluwer Academic Publishers, Boston.

Cook, R. D. and Weisberg, S. (1982). *Residuals and Influence in Regression*, Chapman and Hall, London.

Cootner, P. (1963). "The Role of the Railroads in U. S. Economic Growth", *Journal of Economic History*, Vol. 23, pp. 477–521.

Coto-Millan, P., Banos-Pino, J. and Rodriguez-Alvarez, A. (2000) "Economic Efficiency in Spanish Ports: Some Empirical Evidence", *Maritime Policy & Management*, Vol. 27, pp. 169–174.

Cournot, A. A. (1927). *Researches into the Mathematical Principles of the Theory of Wealth*. 1927 reprint of 1897 translation, Macmillan, New York (Paper appeared originally in 1838).

Cullinane, K. P. B. and Khanna, M. (2000). "Economies of Scale in Large Containerships: Optimal Size and Geographical Implications", *Journal of Transport Geography*, Vol. 8, pp. 181–195

Dasgupta, D., Maity, P., Mukherjee, R., Sarkar, S. and Chattopadhyay, S. (2000). "Growth and Interstate Disparities in India," *Economic and Political Weekly*, Vol.35, No. 27, pp. 3165–3169.

Davis, D. R. (1998). "The Home Market, Trade and Industrial Structure", *American Economic Review*, Vol. 88, pp. 1264–1277

De Monie, G. (1995). "The Problems Faced by Indian Ports Today", *Maritime Policy and Management*, Vol. 22, pp. 235–238.

De, P. (1999). "Concentration of Indian Port System: 1970–1998", *Foreign Trade Review*, Vol. 34, Nos. 3 & 4, pp. 34–43.

De, P. (2003). "Indian Ports in the Era of Globalisation", *World Port Development*, Vol. 3, No. 10, pp. 37–48.

De, P. (2004). "Transaction Costs as Barriers to Economic Integration in Asia: An Empirical Exploration", RIS Discussion Paper No. 77, Research and Information System for Developing Countries (RIS), New Delhi.

De, P. (2005). "Effect of Transaction Costs on International Integration in the Asian Economic Community", in *Asian Economic Cooperation and Integration: Progress, Prospects, and Challenges*, Asian Development Bank (ADB), Manila.

De. P. (2006a). "Total Factor Productivity Growth: Indian Ports in the Era of Globalisation", *Maritime Economics and Logistics*, Vol. 8, No. 4, pp. 366–386.

De., P. (2006b). "Trade, Infrastructure and Transaction Costs: The Imperatives for Asian Economic Cooperation", *Journal of Economic Integration*, Vol. 21, No. 4, pp. 708–735.

De, P. (2008a). "Empirical Estimates of Trade Costs for Asia", In Brooks, D.H. and Menon, J. (eds.), *Infrastructure and Trade in Asia,* Edward Elgar, Cheltenham.

De, P. (2008b). "Trade Costs and Infrastructure: Analysis of the Effects of Trade Impediments in Asia", *Journal of Trade and Integration*, Vol. 12, No. 27, pp. 241–266.

De, P. (2009a). "Empirical Estimates of Transport Costs: Options for Enhancing Asia's Trade", In Brooks, D.H., and Hummels, D. (eds.) *Infrastructure's Role in Lowering Asia's Trade Costs: Building for Trade,* Edward Elgar, Cheltenham.

De, P. (2009b). "Trade Transportation Costs in South Asia: An Empirical Investigation", In Brooks, D.H., and Hummels, D. (eds.) *Infrastructure's Role in Lowering Asia's Trade Costs: Building for Trade,* Edward Elgar, Cheltenham.

De, P. (2009c). "Global Economic and Financial Crisis: India's Trade Potential and Future Prospects", ARTNeT Working Paper No. 64, United Nations Economic and Social Commission for Asia and the Pacific (UNESCAP), Bangkok.

De, P. and Ghosh, B. (2002). "Productivity, Efficiency and Technological Change in Indian Ports", *International Journal of Maritime Economics*, Vol. 4, No. 4, pp. 348–368.

De, P. and Ghosh, B. (2003). "Causality between Performance and Traffic: An Investigation with Indian Ports", *Maritime Policy and Management*, Vol. 30, No. 1, pp. 5–28.

De, P. and Park, Ro-Kyung. (2003). "Container Port System Concentration", *Transportation Quarterly*, Vol. 57, No. 4, pp. 69–82.

De, P. and Park, Ro-Kyung. (2004). "International Container Port System Concentration: What does It Look Like?" *Journal of International Logistics and Trade*, Vol. 2, No. 1, pp. 95–118.

Dixit, A. and Stiglitz, J. (1977). "Monopolistic Competition and Optimum Product Diversity", *American Economic Review*, Vol. 67, No. 1, , pp. 297–308.

Draine, E. H. (1963). "Import Traffic of Chicago and its Hinterland", Research Paper No. 8, Department of Geography, University of Chicago, Chicago.

Dutt, G. and Ravallion, M. (1998). "Why have Some Indian States Done Better than Others at Reducing Rural Poverty", *Economica*, Vol. 65, No. 1, pp. 17–38.

Elhance, A. P. and Lakshamanan, T. R. (1988). "Infrastructure - Production System Dynamics in National and Regional Systems: An Economic Study of the Indian Economy", *Regional Science and Urban Economics*, Vol. 18, No. 6, pp. 511–531.

Engle, R. and Granger, C. W. J. (1987). "Cointegration and Error Correction: Representation, Estimation, and Testing", *Econometrica*, Vol. 55, pp. 251–276.

Estache, A. and Carbajo, J. (1997). "Competing Private Ports: Lessons from Argentina", In: Klaus Tilmes (ed.), *The Private Sector in Infrastructure: Strategy, Regulation, and Risk*, The World Bank, Washington D.C.

Estache, A. and de Rus, G. (2000). "Privatization and Regulation of Transport Infrastructure: Guidelines for Policymakers and Regulators", World Bank Institute, Washington, D.C.

Everett, S. (2002). "Corporatisation Legislation: The Key to the Effective Port Management", Proceedings of the 2002 Annual Conference of International Association of Maritime Economists, November 13 – 15, Panama.

EXIM Bank. (1998). "Transaction Costs of India's Exports: An Analysis", Occasional Paper No. 64, Export Import Bank of India (EXIM Bank), Mumbai.

Farrell, M. J. (1957). "The Measurement of Productive Efficiency", *Journal of Royal Statistical Society A*, Vol. 120, pp. 253–281.

Felipe, J. and McCombie, J. S. L. (2003). "Some Methodological Problems with the Neoclassical Analysis of the East Asian Miracle", *Cambridge Journal of Economics*, Vol. 27, No. 5, pp. 695–721.

Fink, C., Mattoo, A. and Neagu, I. C. (2002). "Trade in International Maritime Services: How Much Does Policy Matter?" *The World Bank Economic Review*, Vol. 16, No. 1, pp. 451–79.

Fogel, R. W. (1964). *Railroads and American Economic Growth: Essays in Economic History*, John Hopkins Press, Baltimore.

Fourgeaud, P. (1999). "Measuring Port Performance", Transportation, Water and Urban Development Department, The World Bank, Washington, D.C.

Frankel, E. G. (1987). *Port Planning and Development*, John Wiley & Sons, New York.

Fruchter, B. (1967). *Introduction to Factor Analysis*, Affiliated East West Press, New Delhi.

Fujita, M. and Mori, T. (1995). "Why are Most Great Cities are Port Cities? Transport Nodes and Spatial Economic Development", Working Paper in Regional Science, No. 175, Regional Science Graduate Programme, University of Pennsylvania, Philadelphia.

Fujita, M. and Mori, T. (1996). "The Role of Ports in the Making of Major Cities: Self-agglomeration and Hub-effect", *Journal of Development Economics*, Vol. 49, pp. 93–120.

Fujita, M. and Mori, T. (1997). "Structural Stability and Evolution of Urban Systems", *Regional Science and Urban Economics*, Vol. 27, No. 8, pp. 399–442.

Fujita, M., Krugman, P. and Venables, A. (1999). *The Spatial Economy - Cities, Regions and International Trade*, MIT Press, Cambridge.

Fuller, W. A. (1976). *Introduction to Statistical Time Series*, John Wiley and Sons, New York.

Gallup, J. and Sachs, J. (1998). "Geography and Economic Growth", Conference Paper, Tenth Annual Bank Conference on Development Economics, The World Bank, Washington D.C.

Ghosh, B. and De, P. (1998). "Role of Infrastructure in Regional Development: A Study of India over the Plan Period", *Economic and Political Weekly*, Vol. 33, Nos. 47 & 48, pp. 3039–3048.

Ghosh, B. and De, P. (2000a). "Linkage between Infrastructure and Income among Indian States: A Tale of Rising Disparities since Independence", *Indian Journal of Applied Economics*, Vol. 8, No. 4, pp. 391–431.

Ghosh, B. and De, P. (2000b). "Impact of Performance Indicator and Labour Endowment on Traffic: Empirical Evidence from Indian Ports," *International Journal of Maritime Economics*, Vol.2, No. 4, pp. 259–282.

Ghosh, B. and De, P. (2001). "Indian Ports and Globalisation: Grounding Economics in Geography", *Economic and Political Weekly*, Vol. 36, No. 34 , pp. 3271–3283.

Ghosh, B. and De, P. (2004). "How Do Different Categories of Infrastructure Affect Development: Evidence from Indian States", *Economic and Political Weekly*, Vol. 38, No. 42, pp. 4645–4657.

Ghosh, B. and De, P. (2005a). "Investigating the Linkage between Infrastructure and Regional Development: Era of Planning to Globalisation", *Journal of Asian Economics*, Vol. 15, No. 1, pp. 1023–1050.

Ghosh, B. and De, P. (2005b). "Infrastructure, Income and Regional Economic Development in India", In: Marjit S. and. Banerjee, N. (eds.) *Development, Displacement and Disparity: India in the Last Quarter of the Twentieth Century*, Orient Longman, Hyderabad.

Ghosh, B. and De, P. (2005c). *India Infrastructure Database 2005*, Bookwell, New Delhi.

Ghosh, B. and Neogi, C. (1993). "Productivity, Efficiency and Technological Change in Indian Manufacturing Industries", *The Developing Economies*, Vol. 31, pp. 308–328.

Ghosh, B., Marjit, S. and Neogi, C. (1998). "Economic Growth and Regional Divergence in India: 1960–1995", *Economic and Political Weekly*, Vol. 33, No. 20, pp. 1312–1321.

Goldar, B. N. (1986). *Productivity Growth in Indian Industry*, Allied Publishers, New Delhi.

Goutheir, H. L. (1970). "Geography, Transportation and Regional Development", *Economic Geography*, Vol. 46, No. 4, pp. 612–619.

Government of India. (1996). *The India Infrastructure Report: Policy Imperatives for Growth and Welfare*, National Council of Applied Economic Research, New Delhi.

Government of India. (1998). *Economic Survey 1997–98*, Ministry of Finance, New Delhi.

Government of India. (1999). *Plan Document: Ninth Five Year Plan (1997–2002)*, Planning Commission, New Delhi.

Government of India. (2006a). *Towards Faster and More Inclusive Growth: An Approach to the 11th Five Year Plan (2007–2012)*, Planning Commission, New Delhi.

Government of India. (2006b). *National Maritime Development Programme (Port Sector),* Department of Shipping, Ministry of Shipping, Road Transport and Highways, Government of India, New Delhi.

Government of India. (2007). *Projections of Investment in Infrastructure during the Eleventh Plan*, Planning Commission, New Delhi.

Government of India. (2009). *Economic Survey 2008–09*, Ministry of Finance, New Delhi.

Granger, C. W. J. (1969). "Investigating Causal Relations by Econometric Models and Cross-spectral Methods", *Econometrica*, Vol. 37, pp. 424–438.

Griliches, Z. (1980). "R&D and Productivity Slowdown", *American Economic Review*, Vol. 70, No. 4, pp. 343–348.

Griliches, Z. (1996). "The Discovery of the Residual: A Historical Note", *Journal of Economic Literature*, Vol. 34, No. 3, pp. 1324–1330.

Griliches, Z., and Jorgenson, D. (1966). "Sources of Measured Productivity Change: Capital Input," *American Economic Review*, Vol. 56, No. 2, pp. 50–61.

Haralambides, H. E. and Behrens, R. (2000). "Port Restructuring in a Global Economy: An Indian Perspective", *International Journal of Transport Economics*, Vol. 27, pp. 19–39.

Hashim, B. R. and Dadi, M. M. (1973). "Capital Output Relations in Indian Manufacturing: 1946–64", M S University of Baroda, Baroda.

Herfindahl, O. C. (1950). "Concentration in the Steel Industry", Doctoral Dissertation, Columbia University, New York.

Hicks, J. (1932). *The Theory of Wages*, McMillan, London.

Hicks, J. (1979). *Causality in Economics*, Basil Blackwell, Oxford.

Hirschman, A. O. (1958). *Strategy of Economic Development*, Yale University Press, New Haven.

Hirst, J. (2000). "Future Management Trends in Australian Ports", Proceedings of the AAPMA Conference PAN PACIFIC 2000, Sydney.

Hoare, A. G. (1986). "British Ports and their Export Hinterlands: A Rapidly Changing Geography", *Geografiska Annaler*, Vol. 68B, pp. 29–40.

Hoffmann, J. (1998). "Concentration in Liner Shipping: Causes and Impacts", *World Sea Trade Service Review*, Vol. 1, pp. 68–74.

Hoffmann, J. (2002). "Concentración y Especialización, sus Causas, y sus Implicaciones para Centroamérica (Concentration and Specialization, Causes, and Implications for Central America)", Presentation to COCATRAM, April 2002, citing *Alphaliner (BRS Shipbrokers Group)*, www.alphaliner.com.

Hoyle, B. (1999). "Port Concentration, Inter-port Competition and Revitalization: The Case of Mombasa, Kenya", *Maritime Policy and Management*, Vol. 26, pp.161–174.

Hummels, D. (1999a). "Have International Trade Costs Declined?", Mimeo, University of Chicago, Chicago.

Hummels, D. (1999b). "Towards a Geography of Trade Costs", Mimeo, University of Chicago, Chigaco.

Hummels, D. (2007). "Transportation Costs and International Trade in the Second Era of Globalization". *Journal of Economic Perspectives,* Vol. 21, pp. 131–154.

Hummels, D. (2009). "Globalization and Transport Cost", Mimeo, NBER and Purdue University, West Lafayette.

Hunter, H. (1965). "Transport in Soviet and Chinese Development", *Economic Development and Cultural Change*, Vol. 14, pp. 71–84.

IDFC. (2001). *India Infrastructure Report 2001*, Infrastructure Development Finance Company Limited (IDFC), Oxford University Press, New Delhi.

Ishikawa, S. (1981). *Essays on Technology, Employment and Industrialization in Economic Development*, Kinokuniya Co., Tokyo.

Isward, W. (1956). *Location and Space-Economy*, MIT Press, Cambridge.

Johansen, S. (1988). "Statistical Analysis of Cointegrating Vectors", *Journal of Economic Dynamics and Control*, Vol. 12, pp. 231–254.

Johansen, S. (1995). *Likelihood-based Inference in Cointegrated Vector Autoregressive Models*, Oxford University Press, London.

Johansen, S. and Juselius, K. (1990). "Maximum Likelihood Estimation and Inference on Cointegration - Applications to the Demand for Money", *Oxford Bulletin of Economics and Statistics*, Vol. 52, pp. 169–210.

Johansson, B. and Wigren, R. (1996). "Production Milieu and Competitive Advantage", In: Batten, D. F and Karlsson, C. K. (eds.), *Infrastructure and the Complexity of Economic Development*, Springer-Verlag, Berlin.

Johnson, D. G. (1950). "The Nature of the Supply Function for Agricultural Products", *American Economic Review*, Vol. 40, No. 4, pp. 539–64.

Juhel, M. H. (1999). "Global Challenges for Ports and Terminal in the New Era", *Ports and Harbors*, March, pp. 17–27.

Keeler, T. E. (1974). "Railroad Costs, Returns to Scale and Excess Capacity", *Review of Economics and Statistics*, Vol. 56, pp. 201–208.

Keeler, T. E. (1983). "Railroads, Freight and Public Policy", The Brookings Institute, Washington D. C.

Kendrick, J.W. (1956). "Productivity Trends in Capital and Labour", *Review of Economics and Statistics*, Vol. 38, No. 3, pp. 248–57.

Kennedy, C. and Thirlwall, A. P. (1972). "Surveys in Applied Economics: Technical Progress", *Economic Journal*, Vol. 82, No. 1, pp. 11–72.

Kent, P. and Hochstein, C. (1998). "Port Reform and Privatization in Conditions of Limited Competition: The Experience of Colombia, Costa Rica and Nicaragua", *Maritime Policy and Management*, Vol. 25, pp. 313–333.

Kent, P. E. (2002). "Monitoring for Port Antitrust Behaviour: An Operational Model and Future Challenges", Proceedings of the 2002 Annual Conference of International Association of Maritime Economists, November 13 – 15, Panama.

Kent, P. E, and Ashar, A. (2001). "Port Competition Regulation: A Tool for Monitoring for Anti-competitive Behaviour", *International Journal of Maritime Economics*, Vol. 3, pp. 27–51.

Kenyon, J. (1970). "Elements in Inter-port Competition in the United States", *Economic Geography*, Vol. 46, pp. 1–24.

Kindleberger, C. P. (1996). *World Economic Primacy: 1500–1990*, Oxford University Press, New York.

Krugman, P. (1979). "Increasing Returns, Monopolistic Competition and International Trade", *Journal of International Economics*, Vol. 9, pp. 469–479.

Krugman, P. (1981). "Trade, Accumulation and Uneven Development", *Journal of Development Economics*, Vol. 8, pp. 149–161.

Krugman, P. (1991). *Geography and Trade*, MIT Press, Cambridge.

Krugman, P. (1993). "First Nature, Second Nature and Metropolitan Location", *Journal of Regional Science*, Vol. 33, No. 2, pp. 129–144.
Krugman, P. (1994a). "Competitiveness: A Dangerous Obsession", *Foreign Affairs*, Vol. 73, No. 2, pp. 28–44.
Krugman, P. (1994b). "The Myth of Asian Miracle", *Foreign Affairs*, Vol. 73, No. 6, pp. 62–78.
Krugman, P. (1995). *Development, Geography and Economic Theory*, MIT Press, Cambridge.
Krugman, P. (1998). "Space: The Final Frontier", *Journal of Economic Perspectives*, Vol. 1, No. 2, pp. 161–174.
Kuby, M. and Reid, N. (1992). "Technological Change and the Concentration of the U. S. General Cargo Port System: 1970–88", *Economic Geography*, Vol. 68, pp. 272–289.
Kumbhakar, S. (1992). "Allocative Distortions, Technological Progress, and Input Demand in US Airlines: 1970–1984", *International Economic Review*, Vol. 33, pp. 723–737.
Kuznet, S. (1955). "Economic Growth and Income Inequality", *American Economic Review*, Vol. 45, No. 1, pp. 4–27.
Lancaster, K. (1980). "Inter-industry Competition under Perfect Monopolistic Condition", *Journal of International Economics*, Vol. 10, No. 2, pp. 151–175.
Lansink, A. O., Silva, E. and Stefanou, S. (2001). "Inter-firm and Intra-firm Efficiency Measures", *Journal of Productivity Analysis*, Vol. 15, pp. 185–199.
Limao, N. and Venables, A. J. (2001). "Infrastructure, Geographical Disadvantage, Transport Costs, and Trade", *The World Bank Economic Review*, Vol. 15, No. 3, pp. 451–479.
Losch, A. (1954). *The Economics of Location*, Fischer Verlag, Jena.
Lucas, Robert E. (1988). "On the Mechanics of Economic Development, *Journal of Monetary Economics*, Vol. 22, No. 1, pp. 3–42.
Mahadevan, R. (2004). *The Economics of Productivity in Asia and Australia*, Edward Elgar, Cheltenham.
Marin, D. (1992). "Is the Export-led Growth Hypobook Valid for Industrialized Countries?", *The Review of Economics and Statistics*, Vol. 74, No. 4, pp. 678–688.
Marjit, S. (1999). "Decentralized Financing, Governance and Public-Private Cooperation", *Economic and Political Weekly*, Vol. 34, pp. 3315–3320.
Marjit, S. and Mitra, S. (1996). "Convergence in Regional Growth Rates: Indian Research Agenda", *Economic and Political Weekly*, Vol. 31, No. 33, pp. 2239–2242.
Martin, R. (1999). "The New Geographical Turn in Economics: Some Critical Reflections", *Cambridge Journal of Economics*, Vol. 23, No. 1, 63–91.
Mayer, H. M. (1978). "Current Trends in Great Lakes Shipping", *GeoJournal*, Vol. 2, pp. 117–122.
McMullen, B. S. (1987). "The Impact of Regulatory Reform on US Motor Carrier Costs", *Journal of Transport Economics and Policy*, Vol. 21, pp. 307–319.

Mody, A. (2001). "Traffic Travails", *Times Shipping Journal*, Vol. 1, pp. 51–52.
Nadiri, M. I. (1970). "International Studies of Factor Inputs and Total Factor Productivity: A Brief Survey", *Review of Income and Wealth*, Vol. 18, No. 2, pp. 129–154.
Nadiri, M. I. (1972). "Some Approaches to the Theory and Measurement of Total Factor Productivity: A Survey", *Journal of Economic Literature*, Vol. 8, No. 4, pp. 1137–1177.
Nadiri, M. I. (1980). "Sectoral Productivity Slowdown", *American Economic Review*, Vol. 70, No. 2, pp. 349–352.
Nelson, R. R. (1981). "Research on Productivity Growth and Productivity Differences: Dead Ends and New Departures", *Journal of Economic Literature*, Vol. 19, No. 3, pp. 1029–64.
Nijkamp, P. (1984). "A Multidimensional Analysis of Regional Infrastructure and Economic Development', In: A. E. Andersson, W. Isard, and T. Puu (eds.), *Regional and Industrial Development Theories, Models and Empirical Evidence*, North-Holland, Amsterdam.
Notteboom, T., Coeck, C. and Broek van den, J. (2000). "Measuring and Explaining the Relative Efficiency of Container Terminals by Means of Bayesian Stochastic Frontier Models", *International Journal of Maritime Economics*, Vol. 2, No. 3, pp. 83–106.
Osterwald-Lenum, M. (1992). "A Note with Quantiles of the Asymptotic Distribution of the Maximum Likelihood Cointegration Rank Test Statistics", *Oxford Bulletin of Economics and Statistics*, Vol. 54, pp. 461–472.
Park, Ro-Kyung and De, P. (2004). "An Alternative Approach to Efficiency Measurement of Seaports", *Maritime Economics & Logistics*, Vol. 6, No. 1, pp. 53–69.
Peters, H. J. (1990). "India's Growing Conflict between Trade and Transport", Policy Research Working Paper No. 346, The World Bank, Washington, D.C.
Peters, H. J. (1992). "Service: The New Focus in Manufacturing and Trade", Policy Research Working Paper No. 950, The World Bank, Washington, D.C.
Peters, H. J. (1995). "Private Sector Involvement in East and Southeast Asian Ports: An Overview of Contractual Arrangements", Working Paper No. PS–10, Transportation, Water and Urban Development Department, The World Bank, Washington, D.C.
Peters, H. J. (1997). "Reforming India's Port System: A Position Paper", Presented at the Japan Chamber of Commerce and the World Bank, Follow up Workshop on the Power and Transportations Sector: India, Tokyo.
Phillips, P. C. B. and Perron, P. (1988). "Testing for a Unit Root in Time Series Regression", *Biometrika*, Vol. 75, pp. 335–346.
Plumlee, C. H. (1982). "Port Performance Index", Transportation, Water and Urban Development Department, The World Bank, Washington, D.C.
Porter, M. (1990). *The Competitive Advantage of Nations*, Macmillan, London.
Quah, D. (1993). "Galtons Fallacy and Tests of the Convergence Hypobook", *Scandinavian Journal Economics*, Vol. 95, No. 4, pp. 427–443.

Radelet, S, and Sachs, J. (1998). "Shipping Costs, Manufactured Exports, and Economic Growth", Mimeo, Harvard University, Cambridge.

RITES. (2000). "Indian Ports in New Millennium: Vision 2020 Report", Rail India Technical and Economic Services Limited (RITES), New Delhi.

Rauch, J. E. (1991). "Comparative Advantage, Geographic Advantage and the Volume of Trade", *The Economic Journal*, Vol. 101, pp. 1230–1244.

Ray, A. (1993). *Maritime India: Ports and Shipping*, Pearl Publishers, Kolkata.

RBI. (2006). "Report on the Survey on Impact of Trade Related Measures on Transaction Costs of Exports", Balance of Payments Statistics Division, Department of Statistical Analysis and Computer Services, Reserve Bank of India (RBI), Mumbai.

Redding, S. and Venables, A. J. (2004). "Economic Geography and International Inequality", *Journal of International Economics*, Vol. 62, No. 1, pp. 53–82.

Reveley, J. and Tull, M. (2008). *Port Privatisation: The Asia-Pacific Experience*, Edward Elgar, Cheltenham.

Rietveld, P and Nijkamp, P. (1993). "Transport and Regional Development", In: Polak, J. and Heertje, A. (eds.), *European Transport Economics*, Blackwell, Oxford.

Romer, P. M. (1986). "Increasing Returns and Long-run Growth", *Journal of Political Economy*, Vol. 94, No. 5, pp. 1002–1038.

Rostow, W. W. (1964). *The Stages of Economic Growth*, Cambridge University Press, Cambridge.

Roychoudhury, U. D. (1977). "Industrial Breakdown of Capital Stock in India", *Journal of Income and Wealth*, Vol. 2, No. 2, pp. 89–102.

Rutton, V. M. (1956). "The Contribution of Technological Progress to Farm Output", *Review of Economic Studies*, Vol. 38, No. 1, pp. 61–69.

Sahai, B. (1986). *The Ports of India*, Publication Division, Ministry of Information and Broadcasting, Government of India, New Delhi.

Sahai, B. (1996). *Indian Shipping: A Historical Survey*, Publication Division, Ministry of Information and Broadcasting, Government of India, New Delhi.

Samuelson, P. A. (1954). "The Transfer Problem and Transport Costs: Analysis of Effects of Trade Impediments", *The Economic Journal*, Vol. LXIV, No. 254, pp. 264–289.

Sargan, J. D. and Bhargava, A. (1983). "Testing Residuals from Least Squares Regression for Being Generated by the Gaussian Random Walk", *Econometrica*, Vol. 51, pp. 153–174.

Sau, S. N. (1990). "Economics of Kolkata-Haldia Port Complex", *Economic and Political Weekly*, Vol. 25, Nos. 18–19, pp. 1015–1026.

Schmookler, J. (1952). "The Changing Efficiency of the American Economy: 1869–1938", *Review of Economics and Statistics*, Vol. 34, No. 3. pp. 214–321.

Scott, A. J. (1987). "The Semiconductor Industry in Southeast Asia: Organization, Location and the International Division of Labour", *Regional Studies*, Vol. 21, pp. 143–159.

Simon, D. (1996). *Transport and Development in the Third World*, Routledge, London.

Solow, R. (1957). "Technical Change and the Aggregate Production Function", *Review of Economic Studies*, Vol. 39, No. 3, pp. 312–320.

Song, Dong-Wook, Cullinane, K. and Roe, M. (2001). *The Productive Efficiency of Container Terminals: An Application to Korea and the UK*, Ashgate, Aldershot.

Srinivasan, T. N. (2000). *Eight Lectures on India's Economic Reforms*, Oxford University Press, New Delhi.

Taaffe, E. J., Morrill, R. L. and Gould, P. R. (1963). "Transport Expansion in Underdeveloped Countries: A Comparative Analysis," *Geographical Review*, Vol. 53, No. 4, pp. 503–529.

Tamaki, D. C. (1999). "Consolidation in the Maritime Industry and its Effects on North American Trade: A U.S. East Coast Case Study", *Ports and Harbors*, September, pp. 12–14.

Trujillo, L, and Serebrisky, T. (2003). "Market Power: Ports", Note Number 260, The World Bank, Washington, D.C.

Tschoegl, A. E. (1982). "Concentration among International Banks", *Journal of Banking and Finance*, Vol. 6, No. 2, pp. 567–578.

UNCTAD. (1983). *Manual on a Uniform System of Port Statistics and Performance Indicators*, United Nations Conference on Trade and Development (UNCTAD), Geneva.

UNCTAD. (1987). *Measuring and Evaluating Port Performance and Productivity*, United Nations Conference on Trade and Development (UNCTAD), Geneva.

UNCTAD. (2001). *Review of Maritime Transport*, United Nations Conference on Trade and Development (UNCTAD), Geneva.

UNCTAD. (2008). *Review of Maritime Transport*, United Nations Conference on Trade and Development, Geneva.

von Thunen, J. (1826). *The Isolated State*, Pergamon, London.

Weber, A. (1929). *Theory of the Location of Industries*, University of Chicago Press, Chicago.

Weigend, G. (1958). "Some Elements in the Study of Port Geography", *Geographical Review*, Vol. 48, pp. 185–200.

Winston, C., Corsi, T. M., Grimn, C. M. and Evans, C. (1990). "The Economic Effects of Surface Freight Deregulation", The Brookings Institute, Washington D.C.

Yap, W. Y. and Lam, J. S. L. (2004). "An Interpretation of Inter-container Port Relationships from the Demand Perspective", *Maritime Policy & Management*, Vol. 31, pp. 337–355.

Yap, W. Y., Lam, J. S. L. and Notteboom, T. (2004). "Developments in Container Port Competition in East Asia", *Transport Reviews*, Vol. 26, No. 2, pp. 167–188.

Young, A. (1994). "Lessons from the East Asian NICS: A Contrarian View", *European Economic Review*, Vol. 38, Nos. 3–4, pp. 964–973.

Young, A. (1995). "The Tyranny of Numbers: Confronting the Statistical Realities of the East Asian Growth Experience", *The Quarterly Journal of Economics*, Vol. 110, No. 3, pp. 641–680.

Index

www.ingramcontent.com/pod-product-compliance
Ingram Content Group UK Ltd.
Pitfield, Milton Keynes, MK11 3LW, UK
UKHW020204290926
15470UKWH00001B/2

9 783034 300056